View of Denning's Point

View of Beacon Landing

View looking north from Bear Mountain

View of Denning's Point

To those who know it, the Hudson River is the most beautiful, messed up, productive, ignored, and surprising piece of water on the face of the earth.

—Robert H. Boyle, *The Hudson River*

Introduction

Diane Shamash

The Hudson River is a powerful physical and imaginative landscape in New York State. From its source in the Adirondacks, to its mouth at the Battery of Manhattan, the Hudson travels 315 miles to New York Bay on its way to the Atlantic Ocean. Its natural geography and history have long been the subject of inspired art, architecture, and literature, well-known through the paintings of Thomas Cole, Frederick E. Church, and Albert Bierstadt, the landscapes of Andrew Jackson Downing, and the Knickerbocker writers. The River's cultural legacy is also present through the estates of its artists — Frederick Church's Moorish Castle *Olana* in the city of Hudson, Jasper Cropsey's *Ever Rest* in Hastings-on-Hudson, and Thomas Cole's *Cedar Grove*, to name a few.

It is well known that the Hudson River School painters, traveling from New York City and elsewhere, helped promote tourism by depicting the Hudson Valley's spectacular mountains, cascading waterfalls, and rocky terrain. Lesser known is the dynamic interplay between Hudson River School artists, prominent industrialists, and the Knickerbocker writers (a name broadly applied to America's first group of literary romanticists working in New York City in the nineteenth century) in the development of a national identity. Promoted by patrons such as Mayor Philip Hone and Jonathan Sturges, and the prose of Washington Irving, James Fenimore Cooper, and William Cullen Bryant, the artists of the Hudson River School helped stir international interest in the Hudson Valley, and more broadly America, as a "sublime wilderness," uniquely American.

Ironically, these artists' efforts to capture the Hudson River's unspoiled wilderness took place as the Hudson Valley emerged as a center of manufacturing and heavy industry. As Thomas Cole and Frederick Church painted the Hudson Highlands, large tracts of wilderness were deforested, and the West Point Foundry exported guns and munitions. Rarely were the 300-pound Parrot guns or iron works at

West Point Foundry visible in the engravings of Currier & Ives and W. J. Bennett, or the paintings of Asher Durand. Hudson Valley School artists and Knickerbocker writers socialized frequently with officers of West Point and industrialists such as Governor Kemble, whose common interest in promoting the virtues of the Hudson Valley drew them together. The schism between art, nature, and industry in the Hudson Valley is still very present, offering residents and visitors unparalleled vistas, as well as waters and ground soil polluted by power plants and PCBs.

14

Watershed was created to offer artists the opportunity to develop new works about the natural and cultural geography of the Hudson River, at a moment when the Valley is undergoing major change. In 2003, several major cultural institutions will open in the Hudson Valley, including Dia Center for the Arts' new 300,000-square-foot museum in the former Nabisco box-printing factory in Beacon, New York. The new Kaatsbaan International Dance Center in Tivoli and the performing arts building designed by Frank Gehry at Bard College in Annandale-on-Hudson will also undoubtedly attract international audiences to the Valley. This cultural renaissance is having a significant impact on depressed local economies in cities like Beacon whose economic base has shifted from manufacturing industries to tourism. Beacon, once a vital manufacturing center known for its brick and textile industries, is struggling to adapt to a new cultural industry that is transforming its empty mill buildings and storefronts on Main Street into galleries and art museums.

Watershed was created to help generate dialogue and engagement with these changing economic and cultural conditions. Participating artists were selected on the basis of their work's ability to reconnect communities to the history and present-day life of cities and towns along the Hudson River, either directly through participatory projects or by increasing public access and involvement with the natural geography of the Hudson River.

A three-year program of commissioned art work, special events and educational initiatives will focus on the 70-mile stretch of the Hudson River between Bear Mountain and Hudson, New York. Art works are supported by an internship program, a journal published annually, and special events, at the region's farms, vineyards, and historic buildings. The goal of *Watershed* is to increase public involvement with contemporary art, bringing together artists and communities throughout the region.

Towards this end, Minetta Brook is working in partnership with many cultural, environmental, and civic organizations in the development of this program. In Beacon, we are working with Dia Center for the Arts and Scenic Hudson to commission a major public art work by George Trakas for Beacon Landing, a 19-acre peninsula located along the Hudson River waterfront. Trakas' sculptural work will create decks, dock areas, and stairways to the water, as well as a landing for small vessels. Also in Beacon, Constance De Jong will create an audio work, *Speaking of the River*, for sound-equipped benches at Madam Brett Park, and Lothar Baumgarten's *Seven rings for contemplation* will provide seating and garden areas at the 67-acre peninsula at Denning's Point.

Artists Christian Philipp Müller and James Welling will engage many aspects of the Valley's agriculture, working collaboratively with local producers. Welling's project, *Agricultural Works*, includes photographs, paintings, works on paper, and audio recordings of farmland, crops, livestock, machinery, and farm architecture. Müller's *Hudson Valley Tastemakers* will trace the tastes from the soil and climate of the Hudson Valley through a cookbook and "earthsculpture" at Bard College in Annandale-on-Hudson.

Several projects will examine the Hudson River's historical and geographical landscape. Matthew Buckingham's film project and symposium, *Muhheakantuck*, will investigate the practices of history and cartography in relation to the Hudson River. Peter Hutton's new film *Two Rivers*, inspired by the third voyage of Henry Hudson on his journey to the Great China Sea in 1609, will include footage of the Yangtze and Hudson Rivers. Matts Leiderstam's project *View* will place binoculars that will locate the landscape paintings of Thomas Cole, Frederic E. Church, Asher B. Durand, and Jasper F. Cropsey in such locations as Bear Mountain, West Point, and Garrison, New York.

Artists are supported by a new internship program developed collaboratively with Vassar, Bard, Dutchess Community, and Marist Colleges, SUNY New Paltz, and Harvard University. This new program, taking place between 2001 and 2003, combines seminars, guest lectures, and artists' presentations with field experience and internships. Undergraduate and graduate students from the Center for Curatorial Studies and Department of Environmental Policy at Bard College; Multidisciplinary Environmental Studies and Art Department at Vassar College; and the Art Department at SUNY New Paltz will work closely with artists on all aspects of their projects.

Watershed's inaugural event will take place at Dick's Castle in Garrison, New York. Dick's Castle, built in 1903, is a 45,000-square-foot Moorish-style castle overlooking the Hudson River. Sitting empty for almost eighty years, the castle is currently undergoing renovation and will open to the public for a rare moment in its history. This event will feature participatory art works, film screenings, performances, and food events commissioned especially for this program. Participating artists include filmmaker Peter Hutton, writer Lynne Tillman, composer Annea Lockwood, and visual artist Pae White. The Dick's Castle event launches the larger *Watershed*, which will open in May of 2003.

As historian Harvey Flad observes in his essay, "The Hudson River Valley and the Geographical Imagination," the earliest descriptions of the Hudson River Valley were travelers' narratives. Explorers, farmers, diplomats, geologists, geographers, historians, writers, and artists sought to describe a pristine wilderness that became central to America's self-identity. Two hundred years later, scenes from the paintings of the Hudson River School are still branded in our imagination, though the terrain is different. *Watershed* brings together artists from around the world to revisit the Hudson River's history, geography, and industries, and in doing so, to offer new narratives to consider. ●

Charles Herbert Moore, *Down the Hudson to West Point*, 1861, Oil on canvas, 19¹/₂ x 29³/₄ inches.

Vassar and Marist College waterfront

View of *Dockside*, Cold Spring

Journal

Miwon Kwon

Three separate journals will be published during the course of the three years of *Watershed*. They are in lieu of a single documentary book or catalogue that summarizes the exhibition as a whole after the fact. While each issue will bear its own identity based on the program's progress at the time of publication. The three journals together will offer historical and cultural background of the Hudson Valley region, profiles of participating artists and their respective works, and contextualization of broader issues relevant to the program.

In addition, the journals will function as a forum for a range of people involved in the program other than the main group of artists. These include students from Marist, Vassar, and Bard Colleges, as well as State University of New York at New Paltz, and Harvard University, who are participating in the educational colloquia (coordinated by

Patricia Phillips); and writers, performers, designers, chefs, and agricultural workers participating in the annual special events program (organized by Lynne Cooke and Sandra Percival). Also, the pages of the journal will be available to artists who are interested in utilizing the space as an extension of their artistic project.

Unlike typical exhibition catalogues, which highlight art works as finished products, the publications for *Watershed* are conceived as a charting of a process that extends beyond the individual artist's shifting concerns over an extended period of time at a given site. Concurrent with tracking such artistic negotiations, the journals will reveal various historical, economic, political, and art historical issues pertinent to the project, precisely as a social process.

23

Village of Cold Spring

Colloquium

Patricia C. Phillips

During the next three years, *Watershed* will bring artists to the Hudson Valley region to develop projects that investigate the cultural and natural geography of this historic and rapidly transforming area. Strategically situated in the center of the region covered by the Project, which encompasses both sides of the Hudson River, beginning at Beacon in the south to the town of Hudson in the north, are five colleges and universities. On the east side of the river are Marist, Vassar and Dutchess Community Colleges in Poughkeepsie, and Bard College in Annandale-on-Hudson. Across the river from Poughkeepsie is the State University of New York at New Paltz. Seeking to stimulate conversation and collaboration between citizens, students, and different cultural, educational, historical, and civic organizations, *Watershed* has developed outreach programs and educational initiatives that foster pedagogical connections and part-nerships between these colleges and universities.

Introduced as a pilot program in summer 2001, the *Watershed* Colloquium encourages students from the region's colleges and universities to become full participants in this multiple-year project. The Colloquium combines a seminar component of guest lectures and artist presentations with field experience and intern-ships. Working with the faculty coordinator of the *Watershed* Colloquium and *Watershed* executive director, students identify the qualities of a meaningful and relevant fieldwork experience. Throughout the summer, each student participates as an intern serving as a liaison with regional, cultural, and educational organizations, works on site in Beacon at the Minetta Brook office, or assists an artist on the research, development, pro-duction, and documentation of a project. A companion to the practicum, a series of seminars serves as a forum for topical and theoretical discussions where students encounter the creative

2001 Internship Program (from right to left) Patricia Philips with Kristen Evangelista, Sandra Firman, Fanny Mariette, Feng Lui.

work and research of artists, as well as the concerns of scholars from different fields and disciplines.

The Colloquium will continue to expand each summer through 2003, opening up to a broader range of students from different areas of study and schools. Opportunities for internships and independent studies will also be available throughout the academic year for students from the region's colleges and universities. Planning projects, activities, and interventions that will unfold over an extended period of time, artists in *Watershed* are working on particular works at specific locations or examining issues related to the region in more abstract ways. Their works raise questions about creative processes, place, community, and different audience experiences and responses to contemporary art. The anticipated breadth of the commissioned artists' ideas, responses, and strategies presents an unusual and promising range of educational opportunities for students and faculty members from Bard, Marist, Dutchess Community, and Vassar Colleges, SUNY New Paltz and Harvard University. •

Special Events

Lynne Cooke, Sandra Percival, and Lynne Tillman

As a prelude to the launch of the newly commissioned art works for *Watershed*, a special events program involving artists, chefs, filmmakers, and writers will take place annually over a weekend during the spring or summer in a unique architectural or agricultural setting in the Hudson Valley. Each year an artist will be commissioned to create an installation with materials or imagery drawn from the bounty of the Hudson Valley and its different produce and "tastes." Culinary indulgence will mark the occasion and the weekend will be punctuated with film screenings, readings, and other events curated by Lynne Cooke, Sandra Percival, and Lynne Tillman.

The first event in May 2003 will take place at Dick's Castle in Garrison, New York. Built in 1903, this 45,000-square-foot, Moorish-style castle is located on thirty-three acres above the bluffs overlooking West Point, the marshes, and the Hudson River in all its majestic flow. After almost eighty years of vacancy, the castle is undergoing renovation and will be open to the public for one of the the first times in its history for this event. The program at Dick's Castle in 2003, featuring art works, film screenings, performances, and food events includes: a presentation of Peter Hutton's epic work, *Study of a River*, a four-part seasonal film of the Hudson River shot over nearly a decade from 1988 to 1997; readings about Rip Van Winkle curated by Lynne Cooke and Lynne Tillman; an audio installation by Annea Lockwood entitled *A Sound Map of the Hudson River*, which charts the 315-mile journey of the Hudson River from its source at Lake Tear of the Clouds in the Adirondack Mountains to the Lower Bay in New York City; and Pae White's design and installation of a series of stylized barbecues and plantings at Dick's Castle to serve as cooking sites for Hudson Valley produce and game, such as corn, fish, onions, and whatever else is good for grilling.

Peter Hutton's films include *Budapest Protrait* (1986), *Landscape (for Manon)* (1987), *New York Portrait, Parts I-III* (1979, 1981, 1990), *In Titan's Goblet* (1991), and *Lodz Symphony* (1993). They have been shown at the Museum of Modern Art, the Whitney Museum of American Art, the Smithsonian Institution, and the Walker Art Center in Minneapolis.

Annea Lockwood is a composer who has worked collaboratively with choreographers and sound poets in the development of multidisciplinary works such as *Glass Concerts* and *Piano Transplants*. Her music has been presented at festivals in New York, Cologne, London, Brussels, Vienna, and Mexico City. She is Professor of Music at Vassar College.

Lynne Tillman, a writer living in New York City, is currently Associate Professional at University at Albany, State University of New York. Her recent books include *The Broad Picture: Essays* (1997), *No Lease on Life* (1998), *Bookstore: The Life and Times of Jeannette Watson and Books & Co* (1999), *Cast in Doubt* (1993), and *The Madame Realism Complex* (1992).

Pae White's drawings, sculptures, and installation works often engage graphic design, architecture, furniture design, and digital media. Her publications include catalogues, books, magazine covers, advertisements, banners, and brochures. She has exhibited internationally at the Museum of Contemporary Art in Los Angeles, the Barbican in London, the International Biennial of Graphic Arts in Ljubljana, the Institute of Contemporary Art in Chicago, and the Fabric Workshop in Philadelphia. •

View of *Dick's Castle*

Lee Balter Interview

Miwon Kwon

Lee Balter is the founding patron of Watershed. This interview was conducted in summer 2001.

MIWON KWON First, I would like to know about your background and how you came to be interested in contemporary art.

LEE BALTER Well, I was a Depression baby, born in 1933. My father died before I was a year old, so my mother had to find work during tough, tough economic times. I worked, too, as soon as I was old enough, delivering newspapers, washing dishes, whatever I could find. There was not a lot of time for art appreciation or anything like that.

Later, after a false start at the University of Michigan's School of Engineering, I graduated from the Hotel School at Cornell University, then worked as a stock trader. Ten years and four children later, I began to realize that although financially successful, I was neither stimulated nor fulfilled by my pursuit of the American Dream. On Sunday mornings I would tear into the arts section of the *New York Times* long before I opened the business section. More years passed, there was a divorce. Then in 1978 I met Nick, a Dutch woman who was an artist and a writer and whose family collected art. We fell in love, married, and bought a wonderful old house in Garrison, New York. Soon we began to buy buildings in Peekskill, a neighboring town and one of the gateways to the Hudson, which had been taken over by crack dealers. We put in a restaurant and apartments, and initiated mixed-use zoning in Peekskill. Our tenant artists' need to show their work stimulated Nick to open a gallery. The first shows were given to proteges of established artists: Donald Judd picked Meg Webster and Carl Andre chose Andromahi Kefalos. I was intoxicated by the energy of the artists. That was nearly twenty years ago.

Shortly before that I had become a director of the Tallix Art Foundry. By this time my interest in contemporary art was cemented. Then in 1991 Nick died of breast cancer. At that time the art market was in a doldrum, causing even top artists to rethink their lives. An art consultant, Joyce Pommeroy Schwartz, introduced me to Robert Morris who was interested in "getting involved" in real estate. Our project never came to fruition, but in the meanwhile Robert had introduced me to the Fattoria di Celle, a sculpture park in Santomato di Pistoia, not far from Florence. Celle was started in 1972 by an Italian textile manufacturer, Giuliani Gori, when he asked four artists if they would be interested in choosing a site on his property and making a sculpture for it. To his surprise, they all said "yes." George Trakas, who is now doing a wonderful work on the Beacon waterfront, was one of the original four. Many more site-specific sculptures have been added since those first four. I return to Celle every year. It has become an annual pilgrimage for me.

MK So did you have the park at Celle in mind as a model for *Watershed*?

LB Celle has been and continues to be an inspiration. But Socrates Sculpture Park in Queens was the model and Noguchi my muse, for it was Noguchi who taught that art should be discovered. And I cannot forget Al Hirschfeld, the caricaturist who hides his daughter's name, Nina, every week in his drawing in the Sunday *New York Times* Arts section. My vision, then: interactive sculpture somewhat hidden in state parks, waiting to be discovered by kids who visit the park.

MK So then what brought you to Minetta Brook and Diane Shamash?

LB A stroke of luck! Our steering committee had made progress to the point of planning budgets and looking for a part-time executive director for the project. At various meetings sponsored by the Dia and Scenic Hudson and Beacon I was impressed by their consultant, Diane Shamash. She was kind enough to meet with me to discuss our needs. Besides giving me some important directional tips, she gave me a list of five possible part-time executive directors. I called all five, reached none, but left messages for all. By the way, you were the only one to return my call. In the meantime, Diane called me and said that she had thought it over and that she was willing to take the job herself. I instantly felt like my dream was finally going to become reality. Diane's taking the job gave the project instant credibility. Literally within weeks, our grand proposal was written and accepted, and Scenic Hudson and New York State Parks had signed on.

MK I know Diane has a rather clear curatorial vision for this program, and it's quite far from the traditional sculptures-in-the-park model. Some of the artists' proposals are very conceptual; some won't even have physical manifestations in the parks. How do you feel about that?

LB I am not trained or knowledgeable enough to be a critic on that point. What I want is simply for park visitors to discover art, which they might not expect to do. And children are uniquely open to discovering things...

MK So you want people to discover art in the parks and, at the same time, the art to draw visitors to discover the parks along the Hudson?

LB I'm not sure that the Parks Department wants to increase visitor attendance to the parks. I don't think the parks are underutilized; they really can't stand a huge amount of traffic.

MK But in the art world, drawing a mass audience is a crucial imperative for exhibition programs. So there might be contradictory drives in terms of attendance.

LB I think what will happen in the parks—if Diane does as good a job as I think she will—is that a lot of different audiences will go up to see the art, creating a new demographic of visitors to the park, including foreigners.

MK Related to that is the problematic relationship between art and urban development or revitalization. In the face of Dia's imminent move into Beacon, there are skeptical voices wondering about whom it will benefit. Clearly, it will revitalize the depressed town in certain economic terms, but what about the displacement of the existing population, the local culture and its history? Have you thought about the social effects of not just *Watershed* but the entry of the international art scene into this region, spearheaded by Dia?

LB Yes, I find it troubling that this "gentrification process" prices out not only the locals, but also the very people who make it happen—the artists. We saw artists gradually move into SoHo and over time transform the area. And now we are watching the beginnings of the remaking of Williamsburg. We've seen the impact of twentieth-century institutions on their neighborhoods—Lincoln Center and the Dia, for example, in New York, the Guggenheim in Bilbao. The New York cultural institutions are not going into wastelands, but into ordinary neighborhoods where manufacturing and commerce are the core. The transformations of Chelsea and the area around Lincoln Center took years and years. But Bilbao is different; the Guggenheim took over the city. The impact was enormous and immediate. Beacon is like Bilbao. Real estate prices have tripled in downtown Beacon since Dia's plans were made public. Vacant buildings that were collapsing and had no takers at any price are being fought over. It's too late now in Beacon, but an interesting model has emerged.

MK What do you mean?

LB Let me try to explain. Years ago I spent an afternoon with Hans Thorner, who developed a Vermont ski area called Magic Mountain. His experience provides the basis for my model. He bought a mountain, carved trails, erected lifts, bringing huge economic benefit to all of the surrounding landowners. But he did not share in the economic benefit that his ski slope brought to his neighbors, and the project was a failure. Before he developed his second ski area, Magic Mountain, he optioned all the land around the mountain, so that he would be a beneficiary of the ensuing economic benefit. The project has been a success for him. The Dia, however, has not learned from its experience. First they moved to Chelsea. Happily and sadly they purchased three buildings. They now occupy two; the third they cannot afford to use because of the high rents they collect. And now they're in Beacon and they've been given an incredible 290,000-square-foot building in need of extensive repair, which they are undertaking—their ski trails and lifts. But now everything that is happening in Beacon is running on Dia's engine. And Dia is not benefiting.

So here is the model. Cultural institutions would borrow state funds guaranteed by the federal government and secured by mortgages on the buildings they bought. For instance, an institution like Dia or Guggenheim might find a wonderful space in a depressed area. Using this pool of low cost funds, they would buy every vacant and downtrodden building around. Some years later, after the economic resurgence, the buildings could be sold or refinanced to pay back the borrowed funds. Then twenty percent of the gain would be used to provide low cost housing to the artists whose move there caused the economic upswing in the area. Profit could also be used to fund projects for the institution that might enrich the education of the local population. So, in my model it would not be the developers who benefit, but the artists and the community.

MK So what kind of hopes do you have for *Watershed* ultimately?

LB In my mind this is a pilot project, and if it is successful, I will endow it. And then I will try to find a Greek Diane Shamash to do the same thing in the birthplace of our civilization.

MK But what is the measure of success that, in your view, will merit an endowment?

LB There are two ways to think about success: one is what I care about and the other is what others care about. Personally, I want kids to experience the project and get turned on by art, in whatever form. Not necessarily every kid, one out of ten would be fabulous. I would like this project to expand people's horizons and interests. I have been enormously influenced by art—learning so much, seeing so much—it's all so exciting. Imagine if you are eight or twelve, how much more exciting it could be. I want to encourage this discovery at an early age. The second part of the success has to do with quality, organization, and environmental impact. Diane has remarkable connections and skills plus a very strong, well-deserved reputation. She probably will be able to avoid and solve the problems of melding art and environment and people with the parks. Stay tuned. It's very exciting. ●

North Dock, Bear Mountain State Park

The Thomas Cole National Historic Site, Village of Catskill

Public Art and Urban Identities

Miwon Kwon

This essay was originally published with the title "For Hamburg: Public Art and Urban Identities" in the exhibition catalogue Public Art Is Everywhere *(Hamburg, Germany: Kunstverein Hamburg and Kulturebehorde of Hamburg, 1997) organized by Christian Philipp Müller. Although my critique here of the conditions of public art and their relationship to urban reorganization seems outdated, reductive, and too strident now, I hope the text will nonetheless add to a richer understanding of the contradictory pressures that impact art programs like* Watershed.

Public art practices within the United States have experienced significant shifts over the past thirty years.[1] The three paradigms can be schematically distinguished: (1) *art in public places*, typically a modernist abstract sculpture placed outdoors to "decorate" or "enrich" urban spaces, especially plaza areas fronting federal buildings or corporate office towers; (2) *art as public spaces*, less object-oriented and more site-conscious art that sought greater integration between art, architecture, and the landscape through artists' collaboration with members of the urban managerial class (such as architects, landscape architects, city planners, urban designers, and city administrators), in the designing of permanent urban (re)development projects such as parks, plazas, buildings, promenades, neighborhoods, etc.; and more recently, (3) *art in the public interest* (or "new genre public art"), often temporary city-based programs focusing on social issues rather than the built environment that involve collaborations with marginalized social groups (rather than design professionals), such as the homeless, battered women, urban youths, AIDS patients, prisoners, and which strive toward the development of politically-conscious community events or programs.

These three paradigms of public art reflect broader shifts in advanced art practices over the past thirty years: the slide of emphasis from aesthetic concerns to social issues, from the conception of an art work as primarily as an object to ephemeral processes or events, from prevalence of permanent installations to temporary interventions, from the primacy of production as source of meaning to reception as site of interpretation, and from autonomy of authorship to its multiplicitous expansion in participatory collaborations. While these shifts represent a greater inclusivity and democratization of art for many artists, arts administrators, arts institutions, and some of their audience members, there is also the danger of a premature and uncritical embrace of "progressive" art as an equivalent of "progressive" politics. (Although neglected by the mainstream art world, artistic practices based in community organizing and political activism has been around for a long time. Why is it now that it has become a favored model in public arts programming and arts funding?) The shifts in artistic practice, while challenging the ideological establishment of art, may at the same time capitulate to the changing modes of capitalist expansion. What appears to be progressive, even transgressive and radical, may in fact serve conservative if not reactionary agendas of the dominant minority.

As a follow-up, I want to address more specifically here the relationship between art practices and the production of urban identities. Throughout its recent history, public art has been defined in part against a (discursive) backdrop of "spectre of placelessness" and the "death of cities." Initially described in architectural terms in the 1960s and 1970s, the ostensive demise of urban centers and the degradation of "quality of life" therein are described more and more now in terms of social problems such as violence, homelessness, poverty, crime, drugs, pollution, etc. But whether concerned with the character of the built environment or with the uneven socio-economic relations foundational to current urban conditions, "place-making" remains a central, if unarticulated, imperative in public arts programming today. Public art participates in the production of a site's distinction, often a city's uniqueness, which in turn is intimately engaged in the processes of economic reorganization of resources and power as they are played out through the rehierarchization of space in the social structure of cities.

I present two seemingly antithetical case studies here to address the art-city relationship. First is Alexander Calder's 1969 sculpture *La Grande Vitesse* in Grand Rapids, Michigan, the first public art work sponsored by the Art-in-Public-Places Program of the National Endowment for the Arts' Visual Arts Program, which was established in 1965. Conceived as a capping for an urban development program, Grand Rapids, like so many other American cities in the late 1960s and 1970s, wanted to build a thriving new downtown business and cultural center. The cultural leaders of the city wanted to "get on the map" both nationally and internationally, which is to say, they conceived the city to be siteless. The city solicited Calder, an artist of international renown, indeed one of the fathers of modernist abstraction, for a work that could be hailed as a "Grand Rapids Calder," like the "Chicago Picasso," which had been commissioned with private funds for the Chicago Civic Center and installed two years earlier in 1967.

Despite the initial controversy regarding *La*

Grande Vitesse over issues of regionalism vs. nationalism, the usefulness of an abstract sculpture vs. a properly large fountain, and questions about Calder's allegiance to America (he had lived in France for most of his adult life), *La Grande Vitesse* in subsequent years has apparently been embraced by the city. Outdoing the Picasso sculpture in its emblematic function, the sculpture has been incorporated into the city's official stationery and its image is even stenciled onto the city's garbage trucks. To the extent that a work of art has become a symbol of the city, *La Grande Vitesse*, as the first public sculpture to be installed under the auspices of the NEA, is still considered to be one of the most successful public art projects in the United States.

Considering the site as a physical entity, Calder's large red sculpture was to become a centralizing focal point, a powerful presence that would visually and spatially organize the space of the plaza, which was modeled somewhat superficially on European piazzas. In addition to providing a "humane" reprieve from the surrounding modern glass-steel office architecture, deemed brutal and inhumane, the sculpture was to function as a marker of identity for the plaza. At the same time, *La Grande Vitesse* was to create an identity for the city at large. On the one hand, the city thought itself to be lacking in distinctive identity, without unique features, a city whose site was unspecific. Harbouring an inferiority complex economically and culturally, Grand Rapids wanted to find a place for itself "on the map." On the other hand, Calder had established himself as a pedigree artist of strong identity and signature style. The function of *La Grande Vitesse* was to infuse the sense of placelessness of the plaza

with the artist's creative originality, to literally mark the plaza site as a singular, "specific" location. By extension, the sculpture was to mark the uniqueness of the city as a whole.

It is important to note that Calder never saw, nor did he feel it necessary to visit, the plaza before the sculpture's installation. Like a good modernist, he operated under the assumptions of an art work's autonomy. The site, in the case of this project, then, was conceived as a kind of abstract blankness awaiting some marker (i.e., art, sculpture) to give it what could be claimed an authentic identity, even if that identity was created through the logic of a logo. The insertion of an art work functioned like an inscription, giving the site a voice. Calder's "voice" as an artist was joined together with Grand Rapids' perceived lack of one, as *La Grande Vitesse* gathered up what surrounds it (the plaza and the city), to become an emblem *for* the city, rendering the city into a sign. In a strange sense, even though the sculpture was not conceived as site specific, it nevertheless became site specific—site specificity was *produced* here as an *effect* and not engaged as a method of artistic production.

Unlike the Calder example, the second case begins with the general cultural valorization of places as the locus of authentic experience and coherent sense of historical and personal identity. Relying on a certain gymnastics of logic in relation to the site, qualities like originality, authenticity, and singularity are reworked in recent site-oriented practices—evacuated from the art work and attributed to the site. "Places with a Past," the 1991 site-specific city-based arts program organized by independent curator

Barbara Kruger, Laurie Hawkinson, Henry Smith-Miller, Nicolas Quennell, Guy Nordenson, Installation view of *Piers 62/63*, 1991, Seattle waterfront.

Mary Jane Jacob, although not conceived as a public art project per se, serves as an instructive example in this context. The exhibition, composed of nineteen site-specific installations by internationally well-known artists, took the city of Charleston, South Carolina, as not only the backdrop but a "bridge between the works of art and the audience."[2] In addition to breaking the rules of the art establishment (taking art to the "street" and to the "people"), "Places with a Past" wanted to further a dialogue between art and the socio-historical dimension of places. According to Jacob, "Charleston proved to be fertile ground" for the investigation of issues concerning

...gender, race, cultural identity, considerations of difference....subjects much in the vanguard of criticism and art-making....The actuality of the situation, the fabric of the time and place of Charleston, offered an incredibly rich and meaningful context for the making and siting of publicly visible and physically prominent installations that rang true in [the artists'] approach to these ideas.[3]

While site-specific art continues to be described as a refutation of originality and authenticity as intrinsic qualities of the art object or the artist,

Pablo Picasso, *Chicago Picasso*, 1967, Richard J. Daley Plaza, Chicago, Illinois.

this resistance facilitates the translation and relocation of these qualities from the art work to the place of its presentation. But then, these qualities *return* to the art work now that it has become integral to the site. Admittedly, according to Jacob, "locations...contribute a specific identity to the shows staged by injecting into the experience the uniqueness of the place."[4] Conversely, if the social, historical, and geographical specificity of Charleston offered artists a unique opportunity to create unrepeatable works (and by extension an unrepeatable exhibition), then exhibitions like "Places with a Past" ultimately utilize art to *promote* Charleston as a unique place also. What is prized most of all in

site-specific (public) art is still the singularity and authenticity that the presence of the artist seems to guarantee, not only in terms of the presumed unrepeatability of the work but in the ways in which the presence of the artist also *endows* places with a "unique" distinction.

As I have written elsewhere,[5] site-specific art can lead to the unearthing of repressed histories, provide support for greater visibility of marginalized groups and issues, and initiate the re(dis)covery of "minor" places so far ignored by the dominant culture. But inasmuch as the current socio-economic order thrives on the (artificial) production and (mass) consumption of difference (for difference sake), the siting of art in "real" places can also be a means to *extract* the social and historical dimensions *out* of places to variously serve the thematic drive of an artist, satisfy institutional demographic profiles, or fulfill the fiscal needs of a city.

Significantly, the appropriation of site-specific public art for the valorization of urban identities comes at a time of a fundamental cultural shift in which architecture and urban planning, formerly the primary media for expressing a vision of the city, are displaced by other media more intimate with marketing and advertising. In the words of urban theorist Kevin Robins, "As cities have become ever more equivalent and urban identities increasingly 'thin,' … it has become necessary to employ advertising and marketing agencies to manufacture such distinctions. It is a question of distinction in a world beyond difference."[6] Site specificity and public art in this context find new importance because they can supply distinction of place and uniqueness of locational identity, highly seductive qualities in the promotion of towns and cities within the competitive restructuring of the global economic hierarchy. Thus, site-specific public art remains inexorably tied to a process that renders particularity and identity of various cities a matter of product differentiation. Indeed, the exhibition catalogue for "Places with a Past" was a tasteful tourist promotion, pitching the city of Charleston as a unique, "artistic," and meaningful place (to visit).[7] Under the pretext of their articulation or resuscitation, site-specific public art can be mobilized to expedite the erasure of differences via the commodification and serialization of places.

It is within this framework, in which art is put to the service of generating a sense of authenticity and uniqueness of place for quasi-promotional agendas, that I understand the goals of city-based art programs in Europe as well, such as "Sculpture. Projects in Münster 1997." (It should be noted that the 1987 Sculpture Project in Münster served as one of the models for "Places with a Past.") According to co-curator Klaus Bussmann's press release,

> The fundamental idea behind the exhibitions was to create a dialogue between artists, the town and the public, in other words, to encourage the artists to create projects that dealt with conditions in the town, its architecture, urban planning, its history and the social structure of society in the town. [....] Invitations to artists from all over the world to come to Münster for the sculpture project, to enter into a debate with the town, have established a tradition which will not only be continued in the year 1997 but beyond this will become something specific to Münster: a town not only as an "open-air museum for modern art" but also as a place for a natural confrontation between history and contemporary art. [....] The aim of the exhibition "Sculpture. Projects in Münster" is to make the town of Münster comprehensible as a complex, historically formed structure exactly in those places that make it stand out from other towns and cities.[8]

Which is to say, the ambitions of programs like "Places with a Past" and "Sculpture. Projects in Münster 1997" ultimately do not seem to veer very far from those of the city officials and cultural leaders of Grand Rapids, Michigan, more than thirty years ago. For despite the tremendous differences in the art of choice among these three events, their investment in generating a sense of uniqueness and authenticity for their respective places of presentation remains quite consistent. As such endeavors to engage art in the nurturing of specificities of locational difference gather momentum, there is a greater and greater urgency in distinguishing between the *cultivation* of art and places and their *appropriation* for the promotion of cities as cultural commodities. ●

1. See my "Im Interesse der Öffentlichkeit...," in *Springer* (December 1996 – February 1997): 30-35.

2. See *Places with a Past: New Site-Specific Art at Charleston's Spoleto Festival*, ex. cat. (New York: Rizzoli, 1991), 19. The exhibition took place May 24-August 4, 1991, with nineteen "site-specific" works by artists including Ann Hamilton, Christian Boltanski, Cindy Sherman, David Hammons, Lorna Simpson and Alva Rogers, Kate Ericson and Mel Ziegler, and Ronald Jones, among others. The promotional materials, especially the exhibition catalogue, emphasized the innovative challenge of the exhibition format over the individual projects, and foregrounded the authorial role of Mary Jane Jacob over the artists.

3. Ibid., 17.

4. Ibid., 15.

5. My comments here are from a longer essay on this topic. See my "One Place After Another: Notes on Site Specificity," *October* 80 (Spring 1997).

6. Kevin Robins, "Prisoners of the City: Whatever Can a Postmodern City Be?," in Erica Carter, James Donald, and Judith Squires, eds., *Space and Place: Theories of Identity and Location* (London: Lawrence & Wishart, 1993), 306.

7. Cultural critic Sharon Zukin has noted, "it seemed to be official policy [by the 1990s] that making a place for art in the city went along with establishing a marketable identity for the city as a whole." See Sharon Zukin, *The Culture of Cities* (Cambridge, MA: Blackwell Publishers, 1995), 23.

8. Klaus Bussmann, undated press release for "Sculpture. Projects in Münster 1997," n.p.

The Hudson River Valley and the Geographical Imagination

Harvey K. Flad

This essay is revised from the volume From the Hudson to the Hamptons: Snapshots of the New York Metropolitan Area, *edited by I. M. Miyares, M. Pavlovskaya, and G. Pope (Washington, D.C.: Association of American Geographers, 2001). I wish to thank the Daniel Smiley Research Center at the Mohonk Preserve and the library staff at the New York State Library for access to their archival resources.*

Introduction

It is as pleasant a land as one can tread upon.

— Henry Hudson, 1607

According to Arnold Guyot, the eminent Professor of Geography and Geology at Princeton University, in an 1887 letter to Albert Smiley, proprietor of the Mohonk Mountain House in the Shawangunk Mountains of the Hudson River Valley in New York State: "Few spots on our continent unite so much beauty of scenery, both grand & lovely, within so small a compass, to be enjoyed with so much ease." (Cited in Burgess, 1980: 22) Here was a landscape which spoke to the geographic imagination. To Guyot and other scientists, travelers, essayists, and artists, the landscape of the Hudson River Valley was at the same time both a fact of natural history and an image that stimulated an emotional response.

OPPOSITE Thomas Cole, *Falls of Kaaterskill*, 1826, Oil on canvas, 43 x 36 inches.

Throughout three centuries of settlement, the Hudson River Valley became a source region for several major streams of historical geographical thought in America. The geographical imagination was enriched through the various narratives employed, which included the fine and applied arts of painting, literature and landscape design to establish this landscape as America's national icon. And it was in attempting to come to terms with the human relationship to this extraordinary environment that many threads in the American conservation movement had their roots.

Early Narratives

The earliest descriptions of the Hudson Valley Region were traveler's narratives. Within the frame of natural history writing, many were simply lists and descriptions of "factual" observations. Published in Europe, they were designed to inform and titillate, much as guidebooks do today for Americans seeking information about exotic lands and peoples. Some were written in an epistolary mode, such as Hector St. John de Crevecoeur's *Letters from an American Farmer* (1782). A naturalized Frenchman, he owned an estate in Orange County—within the Hudson River bio-region. Crevecoeur was a man of science as well as a farmer and, later, a diplomat. He corresponded with those of his day both in Europe and the American colonies on his observations in nature. As environmental scientists of their day, men like Crevecoeur were primarily interested in identifying and recording facts, and they were particularly intrigued by "curiosities." Yet, some of these eighteenth-century observers of natural history became increasingly aware of the interactions of human activities and the natural environment. Before the specialization of the natural sciences into separate disciplines of geology, biology, etc., they could imagine—if not understand—the natural world as a larger system, and it was among some of them, also, that an emerging concern for conservation would develop. Crevecoeur, for example, expressed what can be considered one of America's first statements related to environmental conservation, when he noted the relationship between deforestation and the drying up of the land: "Our ancient woods kept the earth moist and damp, and the sun could evaporate none of the waters contained under the shades." (Cited in Allen and Asselineau, 1987: 44) It would be well into the next century before George Perkins Marsh's writings would help to usher in a scholarly concern about human exhaustion of nature.

Even while writing "useful" observations, however, some eighteenth- and nineteenth-century scientists considered them in teleological terms. The geologist W.W. Mather, for example, introduced his massive 1843 tome on the *Natural History of New York State* with the admonition "... that it may be useful in developing the resources for the State and of our country; that it may lead many to a contemplation of the wonderful works of our Creator, and exalt their minds from nature up to nature's God." (Mather, 1843: x)

By the mid-nineteenth-century geologists and geographers were describing the natural features of the Hudson River Valley in scientific terms. Sir Charles Lyell, in 1841, could carefully describe the Hudson as "an arm of the sea or estuary." These terms remain appropriate, since the Hudson contains both freshwater and salt water, and is tidal for 150 miles to Troy. The source of

Charles Herbert Moore, *The Upper Palisades*, 1860, Oil on canvas, 12 x 20¹/₈ inches.

the river in Lake Tear of the Clouds was not identified until 1872 by Verplanck Colvin when he mapped the Adirondack Mountains. Colvin was later instrumental in having the Adirondacks declared a state forest in 1885 and park in 1892. At over 2,000,000 acres, it is the largest park in the coterminus 48 states, and its wilderness character has been protected by a clause in the state constitution since 1894.

Lyell also described the Palisades as "a lofty precipice of columnar basalt" which, he added, was "extremely picturesque." His description, in effect, bridged the objective and subjective worlds of viewing the landscape. He was quite aware of the language of landscape appreciation of the late eighteenth and early nineteenth century in England. Traveling in the Hudson Valley, he concluded his description: "The scenery deserves all the praise which has been lavished upon it ... it is full of variety and contrast." (Cited in Van Zandt, 1971: 308-09)

Nineteenth-Century Discourse

In nineteenth-century America, the culture's relationship to nature became central to the meaning of national and self-identity. The country had entered the modern era through the economic forces of capitalism and industrialization. Urbanization was creating a vastly different settled landscape, and time and space were

Frederick Edwin Church, *Autumn in North America*, c. 1856, Oil on board, 11¹/₄ x 17 inches.

collapsing under swift technological changes in transportation and communication. A land that had formerly been judged limitless began to suggest boundaries, landscapes of wilderness were being domesticated, the edenic promise was emerging in a middle landscape and deemed of moral virtue.

With the beginning of the industrial revolution and the advent of literary Romanticism, descriptions of the cultural and natural landscape became framed in a new discourse. This aesthetic thematic structure to the narrative would,

over the course of the nineteenth century, infuse nature with social and symbolic meaning. Those trained in this new language were therefore important in the creation of the national argument. Artists in particular emerged as framers of this new vision. Thomas Cole, considered by many to be the primary figure in the development of the so-called Hudson River School of painting, was also an essayist. In his "Essay on American Scenery" he not only presents the elements that are essential for a landscape painting and the emotions that they symbolize, he also forcefully argues for the core of this uniquely American national landscape as being the dialectic between wilderness and the cultivated landscape. He posited: "the most distinctive, and perhaps, the most impressive, characteristic of American scenery, is its wilderness," although he realized, "with the improvements of cultivation the sublimity of the wilderness must pass away." (Cited in Marranca, 1995: 378-79) Other landscape artists, such as Asher B. Durand, Frederick E. Church, and Alfred Bierstadt continued to immortalize the transcendental role of nature in the emerging national consciousness.

The language of landscape appreciation was organized along aesthetic principles that distinguished the "beautiful," the "picturesque," and the "sublime." The former terms could be used to describe both designed and natural landscapes, while sublimity was primarily reserved for a truly awe-inspiring aspect of nature. The search for the sublime was an important part of every traveler's itinerary, and in the early nineteenth century, the "Grand Tour" consisted of traveling, usually by steamboat, up the Hudson River, through the Highlands, to the Catskills, and eventually Niagara Falls. Both men and women made the tour and described their responses to the landscapes they encountered in prose and poetry; they viewed these landscapes as pictorial scenes, rather than as objects to be identified and classified. Already, the language with which mid-nineteenth-century travelers and tourists began to envision nature had been created. The essays and paintings of Cole and his fellow artists as well as the poetry of William Cullen Bryant and the novels of James Fenimore Cooper were largely responsible for shaping the languages of sight and speech among the elite of America.

The contemplation of Nature was likened to meditating on the Creator. One of the most often cited examples of this genre is that of the English actress Fanny Kemble, who wrote of her experience on her trip up the Hudson in 1832 as she hiked up past West Point to the ruins of Fort Putnam to view the surrounding scene. Arriving at the spot, she exclaimed:

49

I looked down, and for a moment my breath seemed to stop, the pulsation of my heart to cease—I was filled with awe. The beauty and wild sublimity of what I beheld seemed almost to crush my faculties—I felt dizzy as though my senses were drowning—I felt as though I had been carried into the immediate presence of God. Though I were to live a thousand years, I never can forget it. (Cited in Van Zandt, 1971: 199)

Landscapes of Tourism

Sublime and picturesque settings were made accessible to tourists who stayed at a mountain house. The Catskill Mountain House, just west of Catskill, New York, on the west shore of the middle Hudson River in the Catskill Mountains, was the most well known of these establishments. Begun in 1824 at the Pine Orchard overlooking the Hudson Valley, this resort hotel became an extraordinary success. It was located within reasonable access to New York City by steamboat and a four-hour stage ride from Catskill Landing up the mountain. Within an easy walk were unequalled vistas, craggy bluffs, deep forests, lakes, and tumbling streams, as well as Kaaterskill Falls, which was second only perhaps to Niagara itself in its fame. Following the lead of their famous artists, lesser painters and poets flocked to the same places to be imbued with the gifts of nature. By the end of the century thousands of visitors a day were making the trip to enjoy luxurious accommodations amidst a wilderness setting.

The landscape they found, however, was not wilderness; it was constructed. Viewscapes, which had been sanctified by artists or writers, were plainly noted in guidebooks and on trail maps; some, such as the view from the verandah of the Catskill Mountain House, became internationally known. From this site, James Fenimore Cooper wrote in *The Pioneers* (1823), the Leatherstocking Natty Bumppo declared that one could see "Creation!... all creation...." Even in 1907, an article in the American Geographical Society's *Bulletin*, predecessor to the *Geographical Review*, could remark that the view from the Pine Orchard site "can easily claim to be one of the most inspiring views of the national domain east of the Rocky Mountains." Here, in the language of geography, we have poetic musing that the view was "inspiring," while political expansionism is apparent in viewing the "national domain."

Naming the landmarks was also a way of inferring an historical or romantic association to the landscape. Both Washington Irving in his Rip Van Winkle stories and Cooper in his Leatherstocking tales began this process of consciously creating a cultural landscape, which was picked up by mapmakers and guidebook salesmen where particular places important to the growing history of the nation were located. In this effort

along the Hudson River particular attention was paid to the Revolutionary War, so that Major Andre's betrayal is always indicated on nineteenth-century traveler's maps. Even in the late twentieth century, the mythological and fictional landscape of Irving and Cooper remains, and helps to identify this region in the national mind; it continues to be marketed in the names of motels and golf courses. Yet, historical association was not enough for a growing national economy, so that even Cole, in seeing the destruction of the wilderness all around him, would argue that "American associations are not so much of the past as of the present and future." (Cited in Marranca, 1995: 383) It would be a theme that would continue throughout the twentieth century as a driving force for conservation and wilderness preservation.

Landscape Design

In 1841, Andrew Jackson Downing published his *Treatise on Landscape Gardening, adapted to North America*. A Hudson Valley horticulturist and author who became the first landscape architect in America, Downing became the "arbiter of Taste" for a rapidly emerging middle class. (Tatum and MacDougall, 1989) In his works he created the language and illustrations which originated the domesticated landscape of home; this landscape became the suburban landscape of the twentieth century, symbolic of America's private domain. One of his collaborators, the architect Alexander Jackson Davis, designed one of the first suburban subdivisions in America, Llellwyn Park in New Jersey, within an easy commute to New York City. Downing also worked on commissions for the public realm. He promoted

"The [U.S. Court of Appeals] held that citizen groups had the legal right, or 'standing,' even if they did not have a direct economic interest, to challenge the potential environmental impacts of proposed construction, and that alternatives must be presented. The court also held that environmental concern extended to both natural and scenic beauty and the historical fabric, not only to the economic cost of a project."

the establishment of parks in cities, which his partner Calvert Vaux would assist in creating after Downing's death in 1852. Vaux teamed up with Frederick Law Olmsted to build New York's Central Park in 1857 and Brooklyn's Prospect Park in 1865. The construction of the first motor parkways in America, the Bronx River Parkway in 1907, is also a legacy of the period.

Throughout the nineteenth and twentieth centuries the Hudson Valley was a contested terrain. Lyell's romantic commentary on the Palisades underscored the battle to preserve the cliffs from being quarried to build New York City's brownstones. They were eventually protected by a society formed in the late nineteenth century that was concerned about the "scenic" value of the cliffs, and eventually formed part of the Palisades Interstate Park in the first decade of the twentieth century.

Preservation, Conservation, and Environmentalism

The preservation of historic sites also was initiated in the Valley. Hasbrouck House in

Mary M. Flad, *Hudson River Sloop Clearwater, Cement Barge, Mid-Hudson Bridge, Poughkeepsie, New York*, 2000, Color photograph.

Newburgh, New York, served as General George Washington's headquarters during the Revolutionary War battles for control of the Hudson River corridor. In 1850 a group of citizens banded together to preserve it as an historic site. By the early twentieth century, federal legislation and other private actions established a national preservation movement. In the region, numerous state and national historic sites were established, which joined together in 1980 with private riverfront estates to form the nation's longest contiguous historic and scenic district that is "as civilized a countryside as we can hope to see," according to John Russell, English art historian and art critic for *The New York Times.* (Cited in Simpson and Flad, 1982: 34)

The industrialization of the Valley had a serious negative impact on the river and its habitat. In 1966, the folk singer Pete Seeger, a resident of Cold Spring, began to conceive of a way to clean up the highly polluted waters. He gathered a group of interested friends to construct a replica of a seventeenth century Dutch sloop. The Hudson River Sloop Clearwater was launched

John H. Johnsen, *Storm King Mountain and Northgate to Hudson to Hudson Highlands*, c. 1969, Color photograph.

three years later, and the environmental advocacy and education organization has become internationally recognized for its successful efforts to bring about positive change. The Hudson River Valley is still a contested terrain in the twenty-first century literally and metaphorically, and the landscape of this place still matters in the debate.

Storm King and the Sense of Place

The birth of the modern American environmental movement may be placed in the Storm King legal case in *Scenic Hudson Preservation Conference v.* *Federal Power Commission*. Consolidated Edison of New York proposed to build the world's largest hydroelectric pump storage facility on the top of Storm King Mountain on the west shore of the Hudson River across from Cold Spring, New York. The preservation society Scenic Hudson, formed in 1963, began a long battle to stop the construction of the plant which would have scarred the mountain, previously represented in the mid-nineteenth-century by essayists and artists as an image of the power of nature. (Dunwell, 1991) The U.S. Court of Appeals decision in 1965 is notable for a number of reasons. It significantly influenced the passage of the nation's major environmental legislation, the National Environmental Policy Act of 1969 (passed January 1, 1970). The Court held that citizen groups had the legal right, or "standing," even if they did not have a direct economic interest, to challenge the potential environmental impacts of proposed construction, and that alternatives must be presented. The court also held that environmental concern extended to both natural and scenic beauty and the historical fabric, not only to the economic cost of a project.

These precedents became significant in the second major battle over a proposed electric power plant in the Hudson River Valley a decade later. A nuclear power plant was proposed in the late 1970's along the banks of the Hudson River within the viewshed of the historic home and studio of the Hudson River School painter Fredrick E. Church. A citizens coalition joined together to challenge the proposal by the utilities, New York State, and the U.S. Nuclear Regulatory Commission.

As in the Storm King hearings, information was presented on the potential environmental impact of the 1200MW facility on the river ecology and the atmosphere, along with consideration for the immense projected costs of over three billion dollars and the economic need for the plant. However, the crucial, and ultimately compelling testimony focused on the aesthetic and visual impact of the 450-foot cooling towers and the associated plumes on the cultural and historic landscape. In both cases, the preservation of the beauty and historical landscapes of the Hudson River Valley were significant factors in defeating the proposals to build large and unnecessary power plants.

Conclusion

By the late twentieth century, the Hudson River Valley had been nationally acclaimed for its beauty and role in American history. According to official New York State tourism estimates, 25 million people a year visit the Hudson Valley, which adds close to $2.5 billion to the regional economy. (Foderaro, 2000) The tourist can still visit the dramatic scenery that inspired Arnold Guyot at the Mohonk Mountain House or the Catskill Mountains that inspired Cole and Church. The River was declared one of the first National Heritage Rivers in 1988 and the Valley a National Heritage Area in 1996. A Hudson River Greenway was established during this decade to link historic and scenic spaces along the length of the River's banks. In 1997, the US Congress declared the Hudson River Valley as the "Landscape that Defines America." As the twenty-first century begins, it is a central place in the national geographical imagination. •

References

Allen, G. W. and Asselineau, R. 1987. *St. John de Crevecoeur: The Life of an American Farmer*. New York: Viking Press.

Burgess, L. E. 1980. *Mohonk: Its People and Spirit*. New Paltz, NY: Smiley Bros., Inc.

Cooper, J. F. 1823. *The Pioneers*. (edited by J. F. Beard. Albany, NY: State University of New York Press, 1980).

Cosgrove, D. and Daniels, S., eds. 1988. *The Iconography of Landscape: Essays on the Symbolic Representation, Design and Use of Past Environments*. Cambridge, England: Cambridge University Press.

Dunwell, F. F. 1991. *The Hudson River Highlands*. New York: Columbia University Press.

54

Evers, A. 1972. *The Catskills: From Wilderness to Woodstock.* New York: Doubleday & Co.

Flad, H. K. 2000. Following 'the pleasant paths of Taste': The Traveler's Eye and New World Landscapes. In *"Humanizing Landscapes: Geography, Culture, and the Magoon Collection."* Poughkeepsie, NY: Frances Lehman Loeb Art Gallery, exhibition catalogue.

Foderaro, L. W. 2000. "Tourism Flowing Upriver to the Hudson Valley." *New York Times*, 21 August, B1.

Howat, J. K. 1972. *The Hudson River and its Painters*. New York: Viking Press.

Huth, H. 1957. *Nature and the American: Three Centuries of Changing Attitudes*. Berkeley: University of California Press.

Lowenthal, D. and Bowden, M. J., eds. 1976. *Geographies of the Mind: Essays in Historical Geography in Honor of John Kirtland Wright*. New York: Oxford University Press.

Mather, W. W. 1843. *Natural History of New York*. Albany, NY: Carroll & Cook.

Miller, A. 1993. *Empire of the Eye: the Cultural Politics of Landscape Representation in the United States, 1825-1875*. Ithaca, NY: Cornell University Press.

Marranca, B., ed. 1995. *A Hudson Valley Reader*. Woodstock, NY: The Overlook Press.

Novak, B. 1980. *Nature and Culture: American Landscape and Painting, 1825-1975*. New York: Oxford University Press.

O'Brien, R. J. 1981. *American Sublime: Landscape and Scenery of the Lower Hudson Valley*. New York: Columbia University Press.

Sears, J. F. 1989. *Sacred Places: American Tourist Attractions in the Nineteenth Century*. New York: Oxford University Press.

Schuyler, D. 1995. "The Sanctified Landscape: The Hudson River Valley, 1820 to 1850." In *Landscape in America*, ed. G.F. Thompson, pp. 93-109. Austin: University of Texas Press.

Simpson, R. and Flad, H. K. 1982. "Preservation of an Historic Rural Landscape: Roles for Public and Private Sectors." In *Farmsteads & Market Towns: A Handbook for Preserving the Cultural Landscape*. Albany, NY: Preservation League of New York State.

Tatum, G. B. and MacDougall, E. B., eds. 1989. *Prophet With Honor: The Career of Andrew Jackson Downing 1815-1852*. Washington, D.C.: Dumbarton Oaks.

Van Zandt, R. 1971. *Chronicles of the Hudson: Three Centuries of Travelers' Accounts*. New Brunswick, NJ: Rutgers University Press.

MIGLIORELLI

FARM

A Rural Life

Verlyn Klinkenborg

A selection of Verlyn Klinkenborg's regular column for The New York Times *is reprinted here with the author's permission.*

28 March

Really provident rural residents are already at work preparing next winter's woodpile. Perhaps it's an unwritten rule of the season: stack next winter's wood before you dig this summer's garden. Or perhaps the splitting and stacking of wood is tied chronologically to the rising of sap in the sugar maples and the sudden appearance of sap buckets hanging in the woods. There is in any case a keen moral pleasure in knowing that firewood split and stacked and sheltered from the weather in March will burn with abandon in November. Less provident rural residents will buy so-called "seasoned" wood in September. They will be plagued all winter long with damp logs and dull fires. When the weather turns sharply colder, their woodpiles will freeze into a single lump.

The lump of firewood beside our house has finally thawed, and an ant—the true harbinger of warm weather—made its way across the bedroom wall and down the page of a book a few days ago. If this time of year is rich in anything, it's rich in expectancy. Everything in nature seems ready to stir, and yet the only thing visibly stirring so far is daylight itself, which is steadily undoing winter. Cold weather has kept the lid on the garden, and the few ambitious shoots that have shown to date seem to be thinking better of it. Ice returns now and then to the small pond in the field. The air looks warm, but it isn't—yet.

What remains most wintry still is the sound of the world at dusk. The chainsaws and axes and hydraulic woodsplitters stop their work, the traffic dies away, and everything is silent. A dog barks in the distance, and a white pine creaks. A train rumbles by just beyond the hill to the east, and eventually the last freight car clatters out of earshot. Then, nothing. The nothingness is audible only because it's just about time to listen for something: the peepers. They'll begin some night before long with a few reedy notes, which will turn, all too swiftly, to uproariousness. Then, it will not be possible to remember the sound of these nights just before the peepers begin. The night sky will suddenly look warmer, more intimate. Orion and Taurus—the winter constellations—will be relegated to early morning. That's the way spring always happens, with a clamorous rush. Humans like to read their own reluctance into the seasons around them. But it's a headlong world in the country, and though most rural residents are provident, not everyone is provident in quite the same way. Some people plan for the winter ahead, and some people plan for the spring.

20 April

When you're on your knees planting an asparagus patch, the mind begins to wander. Asparagus needs a trench, and the act of digging it—

turning the earth with a shovel, scoring it deeply and squarely with a trowel—is a job that sends thoughts scattering like a cloud of gnats. The business of planting asparagus begins to seem very strange, like something out of Poe or something only a child, with a child's native ghoulishness, would relish. An asparagus crown resembles a pale hand with long, withered fingers. With a faint revulsion, you lay the crowns palm-down in the trench and bury them under an inch or two of soil. When they break the surface in a week or two, you bury them again and then again until at last you forget what you've buried and remember only the years and years of asparagus spears to come.

I don't usually eat asparagus, but I've planted it because a farmhouse without asparagus nearby seems unnatural. The same goes for rhubarb and a couple of apple trees and rows of sweet corn and tomatoes. I go down the list of the things I remember from my aunts' and uncles' farms—the pigs and cows, the tractors and machine shop, the dairy and granary, the fields themselves—and I realize that all I can reproduce on four and a half acres in Columbia County is the collection of edible plants that bordered those Iowa farmsteads. That, and the stunning transition from the deep shade of the grove to the blinding openness of a sun-baked pasture. A farm isn't all edges, but the edges it has are always abrupt, at least in the Iowa scheme of things.

There's a Grant Wood painting called *Spring in Town* that shows a bare-backed man spading his garden on the outskirts of an Iowa hamlet. Within the curvature typical of Wood's paintings, that garden is perfectly rectangular, the freshly-dug soil like chocolate pudding. But here in the Northeast, especially in this season, the edges that define the landscape are always blurred. Maple saplings and raspberry brambles smudge the foot of the treeline. Mats of deadnettle blend almost imperceptibly into old quadrants of lawn. In a small reseeded pasture I thought I saw the first signs of new-grown clover and orchard grass the other day. But the green haze covering the bare earth was only sugar maple blossoms.

All distinction seems to dissolve in the soft spring rain that sometimes falls, when the clouds are bright and the earth seems especially porous and receptive. I drove through a farm valley on an evening like that not long ago. On one farm all the Holsteins wore dark leggings of mud. On the hills above them—as rounded as Grant Wood's own—the trees were already chlorophyll green. The overcast on the horizon broke apart for a moment and where there had been many rain-muted colors in the pastures and woods, there was suddenly only the devouring red warmth of the sun.

23 May

For the last few evenings it's been almost impossible to come inside before dark. The shadows deepen and converge, the breeze shuffles the leaves in the sugar maples, and an unappraisable sweetness slips down from the woods—all of it with such careful modulation, the entrance of one player after another, that to call it artful sounds like dispraise. I sit and watch from civil twilight until astronomical twilight. Or, to put it another way, I watch from the time the bats first fly, cutting across the bay of light between the trees that line the pasture, until the bats can be seen only when they eclipse the stars.

But no matter how perfect the night, there is always that voice in my head saying "Come inside." I'm not the only one who hears it. I drive along the farm roads of New York State, and I can see that everyone else is listening for it too. The dairy cows, freed from their stanchions, drift into udder-deep pastures where they'll spend the night. But the farmers have measured the day out in chores, which are nearly always finished under the glare of a yardlight, whose growing intensity is itself a reminder to go inside. A softball game at a rural school is only a way of postponing the dispersal that will come before long, when the last car door thumps shut in the night and the last driver follows his headlights to the highway.

In small rural towns, the voice saying "come inside" is painfully insistent. It's written into the architecture, the landscaping, the principled neatness of the walks leading to each and every house. The azaleas bloom with undimmed ferocity, even in twilight, and the porches are carpeted in plastic turf and set with plastic lawn chairs. In fading light,

unoccupied, they seem to point to the darkness behind the screen door, a darkness broken only by the flickering of a television in another room. Where the houses end, there is nearly always a cemetery. The streetlamps never illuminate that precinct of town. There the good medieval word "curfew" comes to mind, marking the time at night when hearth fires were covered and darkness became absolute.

But on nights as cool and quiet as these have been, why come inside at all? The temptation is to lie out all night listening to the horses, who stand together, head to tail, in their favorite corner of the pasture. "Rigor now is gone to bed," says the spirit Comus in John Milton's masque, "And Advice with scrupulous head, Strict Age, and sour Severity, With their grave saws in slumber lie." Who would choose to join such company? But if you're a mortal reader of Milton, and if you stay outside late enough, you realize that "Comus" is a poem about the real pleasure of coming inside, about fleeing the entanglement of the night, whose otherness feels especially strong the instant you turn for home.

22 June

When the early bird sings at four AM, the only other sound is the dogs running out their dreams at the foot of the bed. Somewhere on the Atlantic the sun is already rising, but at our place the sky at that hour is no brighter than tarnished silver, a superior dullness in the eastern windows.

The early bird is extremely early, and it seems to have perched on the bedside lamp, so piercing is its call. In the phonetic language birders use to represent birdsong, the early bird says, "Why don't—you get—up? Why don't—you get—up?" But at four AM it's all too easy to drift back to sleep. Soon the early bird seems to be saying, in dreamlike fashion, "Guess what—you've just—won! Guess what—you've just—won!" It's worth putting on some clothes and going to find out.

It is 44 degrees outside. The grass is wet with dew. Breath hangs in the air almost as quietly as Jupiter in the southern sky. The early bird, a nesting robin by the sound of it, is stationed in the boughs of a pine across the road. The clarity of the robin's call is a measure of the silence. It will be a windy day, the trees full of their own noises by afternoon, but for now their stillness enlarges the scale on which this solo bird performs. When the robin pauses for a moment, it's possible to hear everything in the world, because there's almost nothing to hear.

Winter mornings hinge on just a change in light without much change in sound. But a summer morning when the sky first glows is a cathedral of anticipation. The choirs that Shakespeare had in mind are neither bare nor ruined, only silent, until one by one, and then all in a rush, the birds fill in. It was never quite so clear before this morning's walk that song is an attribute of light. The birds understand it perfectly. A finch begins to call in a lazy, staccato pulse, the

rhythm of an inexpert seamstress on an old-fashioned Singer. A cardinal starts to spear the air with his voice. Down at the foot of the grape arbor, a cowbird suddenly fizzes and pops. The canopy of trees is answered by the understory, and the tall grasses in the eastern field fill with birdsong too. One by one, the birds add depth to the horizon, until at last there's room for the sun to rise.

26 June

The dogs hear it in the distance before I do and so do the horses, a dry dislocated thump, thunder from far away. One moment there's no wind, the air still and damp. The next moment the wind is turning corners where there are none, lifting and coiling the barnyard dust. Wind flails the leaves on the sugar maples, revealing their silver undersides. It scatters spent hickory flowers in drifts. The sky blackens, and I can almost hear rain begin. But then the wind drops and the front unravels over the western ridge, where the weather comes from. Blue sky intervenes. A clear night threatens once again, Venus hanging peaceful in the dusk.

It's gone on this way for several days in Columbia County, here in the midst of a dry season. Rain promises, and then the cloud cover, which was as tight and dense as a peony bud, blows away in loose tatters to the east. There's no point waiting for thunder to crowd in overhead and for rain to fall. But a single thump sets everyone listening, ready to count the seconds between the flash and the crack of the storm, ready to welcome the hard downpour if it ever comes, though it will cut the garden soil and beat the last of the peonies to the grass.

And yet somehow the need for rain domesticates the very idea of a thunderstorm. Were a storm to blow in now, soaking the earth, it wouldn't be Wagner that ushered the thunder across the treetops and into the clearings, tearing at tree limbs and driving the horses into a frenzy. It would be Rameau, and in the beat of the thunder coming overland there would be something folkish and formal at once, a country dance welling up through the refined strains of an operatic suite.

The horses would circle the pasture in a ground-eating trot, and the trees would sway in some sort of unison, a hiss arising from the new rain on their leaves. I would hear the clatter of the downpour on the barn's metal roof all the way from the covered porch. The Shakespearean undergrowth on this small farm—the dame's rocket and cow-vetch and ground ivy—would twitch under the heavy drops, and the old question of how bees fly in rain would present itself once again.

Only then would something come unhinged in the music of the storm, the lightning moving too close, the shade deepening too abruptly, one of the dogs fetching his breath up short with anxiety. The cataclysm would gradually slide across the valley, and as it did Rameau's music would be heard again, dying away in the east, the

ground sated with rain. If only the storm would begin.

29 July

One of the pleasures in an un-air-conditioned summer is looking at the world through a window screen. During a hot dusk in the suburbs, whole families seat themselves inside screen-tents marshaled on lawns, looking like occupants of the human habitat at the zoo. Are the bugs that bad? Or is there a special pleasure in feeling enclosed but unenclosed, in looking at the world with a new granularity?

There's a screened-in porch on the north side of this house in Big Horn, Wyoming. The screens—10 panels framed in dark green—have decayed over the years. Some have ragged holes in them. Some have sagged, the result of weather and age. But each retains its peculiar power to alter the dimensions of the world outside, to heighten the contrast between deep shade and the full sun on the leaves. When a finch lands on a near bough, it's like watching a Chinese painting come to life, the interwoven texture of the paper visible beneath the brush strokes. When late afternoon arrives and sunlight hits the screens, you can see only the glow of the screens themselves.

A line of saplings grows near the porch, and beyond the saplings runs a creek, and beyond the creek there's a horse pasture shaded by mature cottonwoods. The other night at twilight, as the birds were giving way to

the bats, the robins set up a distracted whirring in the tallest of the cottonwoods. A great horned owl had settled on a bare bough and was calling, with a thin screech, to two more owls farther down the pasture. The screens on the porch had already deepened the night, turning the owl, which was slowly bobbing its head and shouldering its wings up around its ears, into a silhouette.

It wasn't enough, finally, to watch from the porch. To walk out into the open air, down the pasture road, was to recapture the full resolution of the darkening world, to revel in the fineness, the particularity, of sight. The owl in the tree, watching back with a gaze as keen as a dog's nose, was a soft, gray oval, barely discernible from the bark of the cottonwood in which it sat. It cried all night long, as did its fellows, and in the morning they were gone.

18 August

I've been stung by nettles so often this summer that my hands have reached a state of continuous numbness—not so numb, however, that I can't feel the next nettle bite. I go down without gloves to the vegetable garden in early morning when the dew is still thick, planning only to drink my coffee and watch the potatoes grow. But new nettles have always sprung up overnight, and old ones that lay hidden in the hops reveal themselves in the low sun. I can't help plucking them, even barehanded. *Weeds of the Northeast*, that indispensable book, prints a lurid photo of a nettle's stinging hairs. It adds, "When the tip of the hair is broken off on contact with the skin, it acts as a hypodermic needle, injecting the toxins histamine, acetylcholine, and 5-hydroxytryptamine into the wound." Nettles prefer rich soil, so I acknowledge the compliment and heave them onto the compost pile.

On a terrace above the potatoes, a pumpkin plant has wound its way into the sweet corn. So have the vines of the cherry tomatoes, some winter squash, and three cucumber plants—two cukes too many. I step into this maze of vines and stalks every day just to enjoy its architecture and to admire the clutching and grasping going on in the narrow dirt streets beneath the corn stalks. This part of the garden isn't the least bit pastoral. All the vining plants have their hackles up. Their leaves and stems bristle and rasp against the skin as I shift them about, while trying not to step on the cucumbers, which are armored with stiff spurs. The common mellifluousness of spring's new growth is long gone. Everyone in the garden is a character now, for better or worse.

Ripeness is just a form of specialization, or perhaps a specialization of form. Either way, it's descending upon this garden quickly now, like dusk creeping a little nearer every day. It seems like an incredible extravagance to wait so long, so patiently for an ear of sweet corn or a ripe tomato. The wait is nearly over. I almost expect a pause when ripeness comes, but the garden will rush forward into senescence or, rather, into its own definition of ripeness instead of mine. A broccoli has already bolted. The pea vines are stiff and brown. The pole beans have begun to wilt. Japanese beetles have eaten nearly all of the Virginia creeper that steals from the upper garden into the lower one. Only the nettles continue to come up spring-green every day, the nettles, the lamb's-quarters, and the jewelweed.

29 September

Autumn has come, and already the weight of the afternoon sun falls more lightly on my back than it did a few weeks ago. The days seem not only shorter but also somehow thinner too, and every morning that dawns above freezing feels like a morning won back from the inevitable. Nothing is dry yet, of course, but the promise of eventual dryness is in the air. A day will come when every crown of seeds will rattle on the weeds in ditches and fields, when leaves will crunch obligingly underfoot again.

A wet summer is a dark summer, and around here this was one of the darkest summers on record. In fact, darkness was about 10 inches above normal in the Albany area by the time autumn began. Never were the fungicidal qualities of exterior paint more highly prized than during this summer past. Old wooden barns and outbuildings became studies in parasitism. In our bedroom, a mushroom the size of a child's head sprouted from an interior beam. All in all, it was a good summer to be an epiphyte from one of the gloomier, more downcast species.

But as autumn advances, the woods will open up again. The deep shade, which seemed so unfamiliar when it first returned in late spring, will dissipate. Antiseptic sunlight will again reach the waterlogged earth beneath the great stands of oak and maple. Even as daylight slackens, week by week, the turning, yellowing leaves will reflect more light at wavelengths with a warm, inviting cast. As the leaves cover the ground, the floor of the deciduous forest will begin to throw light upwards toward the sky. The landscape will seem to decrease in volume because the woods are bare.

What all of this means is that the catbird will be leaving soon. It's lived in the green shade beside a rotting porch all summer long. I glimpse it only now and then—a slender gray bird wearing a black skullcap, scratching among the lower branches along the edge of the woods. When it calls, it doesn't sound like a cat meowing. It sounds like an imitation of a cat meowing, like a squirrel throwing its voice in order to puzzle a dog. But when it sings, the catbird distills shadows into music, the way the nightingale does in English poetry. There's a faintly mechanical quality to its song, as though the notes were produced by small bells or the operation of intricate machinery. When the woods open up and there is no shade left to hide it, the catbird will go. Summer will finally have come to an end.

24 October

On a warm October afternoon, high in a sugar maple, a crow disemboweled a hornet's nest, discarding shreds of gray hornet-paper like leaves in a monochrome fall. A hail of ladybugs rose and then fell against the south side of the house. They were hapless fliers burdened by ungainly wing-covers, clattering almost inaudibly against the parched siding, seeking cracks and lifted clapboards to winter under. The sight of so many ladybugs in flight, each one armed with a faint acrid stench, looked like the threat of a hard season coming. When that many creatures take shelter at once, you wonder what they're sheltering from. Soon we'll know.

The woods are luminous, brighter somehow where the maples stand against a backdrop of unchanging hemlock. Even as light leaks out of the month, the woods seem to compensate, opening again to the western horizon. The sun has made its way southward like the fox that crosses the pasture most evenings. The air wears the tannic acidity of decaying leaves. The suppleness of light just when it fades in late afternoon seems almost mocking. It's a humiliating display of color, towering out of the treetops and into the backlit clouds overhead. At twilight, my wife found a newly killed male cardinal lying in the grass, its head severed by one of our cats. There was nothing in the day so sharply defined as the line where the black around its bill met the red of its crest, nothing so autumnal as the grief it aroused.

That morning, I had lit a brush-pile on fire. There was a raucous half-hour, when the flames seemed to catch at something inside me. Then the fire settled down to business, smoldering steadily, adding its own taint to the air. Crab-apple leaves on boughs cut a day earlier shriveled like a time-lapse glimpse of late autumn. The fruit sizzled and dropped into the flames. It seemed hard to believe, a couple of hours later, that a pile so rampant could now be nothing more than a small mound of ash.

After twilight had come and gone and the temperature had dropped, I walked down again to where the bonfire had been. I turned the ashes with a manure fork. A night breeze blew across the coals and reddened them. They seemed to ripple in the darkness, their light refracted by their heat. For a moment I stood beside them, taking in their warmth. And then I was lost in an illusion. That array of unsteady lights looked like the fires of some ancient city seen from high above, a place described by Goethe long ago, when he wrote, "The king is out hunting, the queen is expecting a child, and so things could not be better."

30 October

When snow began falling on Sunday, I realized that a line from Keats—"until they think warm days will never cease"—had been running through my head for weeks. The line is from his ode "To Autumn," one of the loveliest poems in the language, and

"they" are the bees, whose clammy cells, as Keats calls their comb, have been "o'erbrimm'd" by summer. Jonathan Bate, author of a new book called *The Song of the Earth* observes that the late summer of 1819, the season leading up to the completion of Keats' ode on Sept. 19, "was clear and sunny on thirty-eight out of the forty-seven days from 7 August to 22 September 1819" and that temperatures were milder in the final week of that period than they had been in three years.

This wasn't merely a spate of beautiful weather. It was weather of a kind, Bate notes, that would actually make breath come easier for a consumptive like Keats. There could be nothing more personal than the question of Keats' lung capacity, and yet "To Autumn" does not read as a personal poem. There is, it's true, something deceptively long-winded in the syntax of the first stanza, and some critics have seen a consumptive's hectic flush in the stubble plains touched with "rosy hue." But Mr. Bate reminds us, too, how broad the boundaries of "personal" experience really are. For Keats, those boundaries include the season as a whole. The fine weather o'erbrimm'd him, and in doing so gave voice to itself.

Until the past few days, it was a Keatsian autumn, full of what the poet calls, in a letter from those same weeks, "Chaste weather—Dian skies." Never mind that the leaves are now almost gone, or that the skies are now unchaste, gray and dousing us with snow showers. Somehow the brightness of the trees

created the illusion that the periphery of one's awareness had expanded. When we walked the dogs, it felt as though we were all walking with eyebrows raised, though for the dogs that would be with nostrils distended.

Keats personified autumn, imagining her by a cider press or fast asleep in a "half-reap'd furrow." Personifying the natural world is so fundamental and so limitless that it seems sometimes like the foundation of all poetry. To some, I suppose, personifying nature appears to be an act of hubris, a refusal to accept the otherness of the world around us. But in a fall like this one—dry after a long wet, warm after unusual coolness—personifying nature seems only like a means of meeting nature halfway. In the ghostliness of Keats' autumn, "sitting careless on a granary floor," what we really see is the way the season swells within us.

20 November

This time of year the light is always coming and going. Dawn swells until noon, and then, after a brief hesitation, twilight takes over. The sun edges around the day like a fox making homeward tracks along the margin of a snow-covered field. Summer, in memory, seems almost like a plain of sunshine, without undulation. There's an astronomical explanation for it all—the sun cuts a much lower angle across the sky in late autumn and sets farther south. But it's simpler to say that at this time of year, in the country at least, emotion and light are one and the same.

This is never truer than on a dark November morning, well before sunrise. A few days ago a freezing rain fell. The day began with the clatter of ice pellets against the windows. It sounded like crows dancing on the skylight. The falling ice was colorless, almost invisible against the thicket of bare woods. But by evening the freezing rain had turned to snow, and before long six inches had fallen over a glaze of ice.

By early Monday morning, the balance of light had changed completely. All the dark, difficult textures of earth—the matted bogs, the abraded fields—had been smoothed over, simplified. What seemed before to entangle the light now reflected it. Even at 5:30 on an overcast morning the snow seemed to phosphoresce, to reveal the broad contours of the landscape while concealing its subtlest variations. Even in darkness a driver could sense the snow-lit dimension of the long north-south corridors of Columbia County.

In the valley that Route 22 follows, each light seemed to weigh in with a different mood. Halogen lamps on a weekend estate picked out every coruscation in their field of view. The kitchen windows of a farmhouse burned with an old-fashioned, amber glow. Beyond the farmhouse shone a long bank of lights—the windows of a milking parlor filled with cows grazing at their stanchions, the hiss of the milking machines almost audible in the silence outside, where the barn threw its light on the snow.

1 December

In late August, what snow remains along the ridgelines of the Madison Range, in southwestern Montana, is as gray as a cast antler, and it has the porosity of cruelly weathered bone, almost eaten away by sun and wind and age. Still, it's hard not to think of those snowfields as the nucleus from which winter will come, spreading downward in the night, taking the unprepared unawares and bestowing a kind of small-town smugness on those who have their snowblowers and skis tuned up in July. Seasonal morals—think of the grasshopper and the ant—echo down through folk literature, through the commonplaces of our tongue, but no season carries a sterner moral than winter, and what makes it so is snow.

Some people love waking to the sight of new snow. Fallen snow is fine, but I like the sight of it falling, fine as dust or so fat you can hear it land against the kitchen window. I like the tunnel of dry snow into which you drive at night, the headlights blanking out a few yards ahead, and the feeling that you're driving into some abyssal vacuum. I like the ground-blizzards and the snow that slithers down the road ahead of you. What I like is the visual impairment snow brings with it, the way it obscures some things and clarifies others, like the wind, whose conformities snow reveals.

My grandmother Carley always used to say to me, when I was in one of my childhood snow-reveries, "You won't feel that way when you're my age." I'm halfway there now, and

nothing's changed. I suppose that some day I'll feel tyrannized by snow, but the truest and the most consistent of all the feelings I've ever felt is the one I feel when I look up, on a gray day in November, and see that out the window the air has filled with snow, snow as still, as hesitant, as the motes of dust in a morning sunbeam. It reminds me of a classroom in an old brick schoolbuilding. There was only one small window, mounted high on the wall near the top of a set of stairs that led down to a dank gymnasium. Through that high window I could see the boughs of some conifer, a Douglas fir or a Norway spruce. Whenever snow begins to fall, wherever I am, I'm in that room again, watching the flakes balanced in the air against the dark green boughs, waiting for them to thicken and gain impulsion and for the wind to multiply them until the snow is so thick that the tree fades from sight, and we're sent home early and the snow fills in our tracks so swiftly that it's doubtful we'll ever find our way back to school, not tomorrow or the day after or for weeks to come.

28 December

The high ground in Columbia County has been covered with snow since mid-November. Every cold night the snow tenses, and every warm day it relaxes, sponging moisture into the still-unfrozen soil. At our place, the horses have strewn a green carpet of hay underfoot, and two crows feed at its edge. The snow has buried nearly everything in that pasture, but what it

hasn't buried it has thrown into silhouette, denuding it of color. The tops of the tallest grasses and weeds protrude from the whiteness, their shapes revealed with peculiar clarity. On sharp days when there has been light wind and a new inch or two, the weed stems cut a V in the snow. When the wind has been especially strong, the weed tops—their inflorescences—leave a distinctive print, a brushmark, on the surface.

Snow makes a miniaturist of almost anyone who walks through the fields this time of year. An abandoned clearing that was full of color in August or June now displays the remnants of only a few plants, stiff, skeletal forms still bearing seed against the spring. The blankness of the background confers a kind of unaccustomed grandeur on some of the plants that still stand upright. Burdocks—most grasping, most contemptible of weeds—spread like ancient oaks. Galls appear like minarets high on a clump of weedstalks. Goldenrods bend as though they were seaweed swayed by a light current. The ingenuity, the evolutionary virtuosity of botanical design becomes apparent among the motherwort, a plant with carillon after carillon of empty, spiny bells surrounding its four-sided stalk.

In late December, the eye feels an almost painful hunger for light. The open woods, bereft of leaves, and the snow itself feel like a kind of appeasement, a way of making amends to the eye for the almost grudging tread of the sun across the sky. It is that hunger that makes the

detail of the natural world so precious now. Pale green lichen on a sodden tree trunk has all the power of a daylily in bloom. Where moss insulates a south-facing rock outcrop, a few ferns still remain Maygreen. The color, like the very plushness of the moss, seems almost inconceivable. It's tempting to think of winter as the negation of life, but life has too many sequences, too many rhythms to be altogether quieted by snow and cold. Why are there still leaves on the maple boughs that snapped off in a big storm this autumn? How does it happen that midges hatch on a day just slightly warmer than the rest of the week? They rise from a brook and follow its course upstream, into the darkness of a hemlock wood.

8 January

All of the days with eves before them are behind us now for another year. The grand themes—rebirth and genial carnality—have come and gone like a chinook wind, bringing a familiar end-of-year thaw to body and spirit. Now the everyday returns, and with it the ordinary kind of week in which Friday doesn't turn into Sunday—and Saturday into Sunday—as it has for two weeks running. It's time for a week in which each morning throws off a magnetic field all its own, when it's no trick telling Tuesday from Wednesday just by the sound of the alarm clock or the mood of your spouse.

With the everyday, winter comes at last to the new year. In the country,

it isn't necessarily snowfall that marks the return of winter nor the sudden drop in temperature. It's the sound of the plow-guy—unless you happen to be the plow-guy—clearing the driveway well after dark, when the dogs are already asleep, too tired from an afternoon of running around a snowy field to rise and bark at the scraping and banging outside. In the time it takes to wonder what the racket is, I remember. It was last winter's sound and now it's this winter's too. It seems surprising that the plow-guy even recalls where I live and that such a flimsy agreement—a couple of words and a nod over a rolled-down pickup window—could have such presumptive force. But that's the nature of the country, where life-long service contracts are formed in an instant and attach to the property, not the person, as newcomers discover to their interest. Getting out of those contracts is like getting out of winter. Better just to move.

Winter's own presumptive force made itself plain recently, with rain upon snow followed by snow upon ice late into the darkness. The next morning my footsteps to the barn through the slush the night before had been preserved with remarkable sharpness—each one a life-mask of my boot-sole, the splash frozen in mid-air like a Harold Edgerton photo. In the sunshine, snow slid off the metal barn-roof with a hiss, and the horses skittered out from the run-in shed, taking pleasure, as they always seem to do, in a momentary fright, having found out, in a single night, how to pick their way over ice again.

The roads are suddenly full of the over-tentative and the over-bold, for at night the cold, clean blacktop looks like hardpacked snow, and sometimes it actually is. Other seasons come abruptly but ask so little when they do. Winter is the only one that has to be relearned.

20 January

The deep cold we've been having these past few days is inherently silent, of course. But if it made a sound it would be the scissoring and gnashing of a skater's blades against hard gray ice, or the screeching the snow sets up when you walk across it in the blue light of afternoon. The sound might be the stamping of feet at bus-stops and train-stations, or the way the almost perfect clarity of the audible world on an icy day is muted by scarves and mufflers pulled up over the face and around the ears.

But the true sound of deep cold is the sound of the wind. Monday morning, on the streets of Cambridge, Massachusetts, the wind-chill approached 50 below zero. A stiff northwest wind rocked in the trees and snatched at cars as they idled at the curb. A rough rime had settled over that old-brick city the day before and now the wind was sanding it smooth. It was cold of Siberian or Antarctic intensity, and I could feel a kind of claustrophobia settling in all over Boston as people went about their errands, only to cut them short instantly, turning backs to the gust and fleeing for cover.

It has been just slightly milder in New York. Furnace repairmen and oil-truck drivers are working on the memory of two hours sleep. Swans in the smaller reservoirs brood on the ice, and in the swamps that line the railroad tracks in Dutchess County, you can see how the current was moving when the cold snap brought it to a halt. The soil in wind-blown fields looks—and is—iron-hard. It's all a paradox, a cold that feels absolutely rigid but which nonetheless seeps through ill-fitting windows, between clapboards, and along uninsulated chases of pipe. People listen superstitiously to the sounds in their heating ducts, to the banging of their radiators, afraid of silence. They turn the keys in their cars with trepidation. It's an old world this cold week, a reminder of years ago when snow was deeper, winter was longer, and, somehow, it all seemed just right.

23 February

From a distance, the woods in winter look monochromatic, gray with undertones of dull red and olive, as if all the trees were a single species. For anything I knew until recently, they might have been. Most of my life, I have wandered through a forest of gross generalization, able, in summer, to tell an oak from a maple and a pine from a birch but unable to make any finer distinctions among them. I have a useless scattering of arboreal knowledge, which for some reason I've never troubled to refine. Eucalyptus, magnolia, manzanita, madrone, juniper, pinyon, even

acacia—each of these I recognize, but none of them grows native in the woods around me in Columbia County. What does grow here, I've been able to say rather grandly till now, are trees.

But I awoke recently with a deep taxonomic yearning, an urge to sort the trees in the forest by name. I've found, for instance, that on the east side of the house I live in there are two pignut hickories, enormous, stately trees. Beneath one of them grows a hemlock, a reminder that hemlock is highly tolerant of shade. Until this weekend I had never turned over a hemlock needle and noticed the two white lines that identify it. On the rocky slope north of the house, there are more hemlocks, and compatriot beeches too, elegant, smooth-barked trees surrounded by their juniors, bearing tightly-furled buds on the tips of their boughs. The old barbed-wire fence that surrounds the barnyard was strung along a line of black birches, which grow, the naturalists say, on disturbed ground and which have long since embosomed the wire and staples. Up the hill from an old railroad reservoir, there's a stand of paper birches, on one of which a great sheet of bark has come unpeeled, ready for the presses. Still farther up that hill, in a clearing overgrown with brambles, there's a solitary white pine, whose name I know only because its needles grow five to a bunch.

That's the kind of knowledge you carry into the woods when you first begin classifying—the fundamental keys that allow you to cleave one tree from the mass and call it Fagus grandifolia or Betula papyerifera. Perplexing as the woods can be at times, there's an underlying order to them. Do the buds on a twig, or the twigs on a bough, grow opposite one another? Then it can't be an oak or a hickory. Do the buds alternate along the twig? Then it can't be a maple or an ash. Spruce needles are square and can be rolled between the fingers. Fir needles are flat and can't be rolled. There's something appealing, especially on a gray winter afternoon, about learning such basic things. Walking through the woods with these keys in hand resembles the summer I learned the stars. Night after night I sat up into the early morning, sorting through the constellations and learning something about their movement through the sky. It wasn't enough knowledge to let me navigate the heavens, but it was enough to make me feel at home on earth.

6 March

Just about now a certain winter-weariness sets in, at least for those of us who live in the country. Every morning and evening you can feel the sun pushing back the margins of night, and it's a dull soul who hasn't checked sunrise or sunset against his watch several times by now, struck by how early the light comes and how late it begins to go. But that just makes a day of heavy overcast and freezing rain feel all the worse, more of an impairment than it would have been when the sodden year was still shrinking. The rain falls as it has all winter, over ice and snow, as if to make a none-too-subtle point about the climate in this part of New York State, a point that those of us who live here start to take seriously only about now.

The rain falls on frozen ground, and the barnyard looks medieval, a vile compost tea brewing in every puddle. Where the bird feeders hang, it looks as though we're running a goldfinch feedlot. Sullen birds shoulder each other aside and seem to squabble more than finches ordinarily do, which is constantly. The other day a mob of robins appeared in the lower pasture on a southeastern slope where the ice cap had retreated. They moved like shore birds across the frozen turf, staggering forward and falling back, not just that lone bird—the first robin, sign of spring—but a herd, as though there wouldn't be enough assurance in the sight of only one.

I filled the horses' water tank the other morning, and as I did a pileated woodpecker cut across the hillside with a cry of demented hilarity. On dry, cold mornings, the woodpecker goes to work at early light knocking a row of holes in a hollow tree trunk, waking the woods from hibernation, raising the sap in the sugar maples. The pileated woodpecker forecasts nothing, as far as I can tell. It lives here year round, and its plumage doesn't seem to change, nor does its lunatic cry. Before long, the woodpecker will begin trying to drill through the metal roof of the

barn the way it did last year. It will sound as though the world were an empty 55-gallon drum with only the bird on the outside, hammering away. The racket puzzles even the crows in the ash trees, and they're foxed by nothing.

One day soon the rain will let up, and the frost will leave the ground as stealthily as it came. There will be yielding all around and a sudden insistent adhesion in the barnyard. The urge to clean away winter from the corners of the lawn, from the deep shade beneath the hemlocks, will become irresistible. But all of this hides somewhere on the next page of the calendar. The good news now lies deep within the beehive, where the workers, their dead cast aside into the melting snow, have set the queen laying eggs once again.

16 March

It's been as ugly here, two and a half hours north of New York City, as open, undisturbed country ever gets. One day early last week the temperature reached 47° in the afternoon, with steady rain. The ground was frozen and still partly covered by snow, which had turned porous and grainy. A dense vapor clung to the

tops of the snowbanks. Water ran in thin, scalloped rivulets across tarred roads. It streamed across the earth and pooled in every depression, where it stayed because it had nowhere to go. In every ditch, every hollow, a tea was steeping, a cold, sepia tea of last year's leaves in a basin of discolored ice. It was easy to find yourself staring into the tangled woods, wondering why exactly humans had never learned to hibernate and whether it was too late to think again.

There's a limit to how ugly Manhattan gets in that kind of weather. The light can only fail so far in the rain before buildings begin to glisten. The city never feels quite so immense, or so familiar, as when the fog closes in. But on a cold, wet night here on the edge of the woods, the opacity is shocking. This isn't the deep sky darkness of December or January, when the emptiness of space seems to reach right down to the horizon. This feels like some suffocating, damp antithesis.

And still, a few days ago, the ground was frozen solid. On late October mornings, when the grass suffers a brittle frost, the earth remains soft, though you can feel it tightening underfoot. Now conditions were reversed. In the fields, the long

grass looked like Ophelia's hair, caught by the current in which she drowned. Yet there was nothing pliant about the earth to which it was rooted. No give at all.

On Thursday, all at once, the soil would take the print of a foot. Not a deep print. As I walked, I could feel a thin layer of soil sliding over the frost-bound dirt beneath it, like the flesh of the forehead over the skull. By the weekend, it was treacherous walking, mud over shoes in the wet spots. On drier ground, there was suddenly a remarkable sense of leniency. The soil felt almost buoyant, like a gymnast's mat. It invited a fall.

You often hear mud season reviled up here, though no one really misses a bitter winter like this one now passing into memory. In these tentative days at the end of February and the start of March, people talk as though the snow were simply in remission. But when the frost starts to go out of the ground, when even a day with heavy fog holds the light longer than a clear day in late December, you realize that you've thought of winter all along as the still point in the rotation of the seasons. Well, nothing is still any longer. This corner of the planet is melting, and we'll be up to the axles in it any day now.

Nancy McNamara, Honey Locust Farm, Newburgh, New York

Lothar Baumgarten, Installation view of *AMERICA Invention*, 1993, Guggenheim Museum.

Lothar Baumgarten

George Baker

Lothar Baumgarten is perhaps best known in this country for having inscribed the names of the indigenous peoples of North and South America along the entire length of the Guggenheim Museum's spiral in 1993. *AMERICA Invention*, he called it, as the names marched down the length of the museum's walls, slowly spinning: TLINGIT, HEIDA, TSHIMSHIAN, ALGO-NQUIN, OJIBWAY, IROQUOIS. But this project was simply the culmination of many other such public inscriptions completed since the 1970s, from his 1982 *Monument for the Indian Nations of South America* emblazoned around a skylight in the Fridericianum in Kassel, Germany (...TUPINAMBA, BORORO, XAVANTE, TOBA, AREKUNA...), to his more recent exhibition at MOCA in Los Angeles entitled *Carbon*, an investigation of the history of the railroad in North America and its effects upon indigenous populations (...APACHE, CHEYENNE, TETON, ARAPAHO, PAWNEE...).

The American critic Craig Owens once claimed that these names were Baumgarten's "medium," the only unity in an artistic practice irreducibly fragmented between Western museum installations and travel in the South American rainforest, between site-specific exhibitions and book publications, between the media of film, photography, slide projection, text, and sculpture. Unlike the seemingly parallel use of names in public monuments such as Maya Lin's Vietnam Memorial, Baumgarten's inscriptions are not simple memorials. They may seem elegiac, evoking memories of that which has been lost. But that is only part of their aesthetic power. "These names are polyphonic," Baumgarten has written. "They talk back to us about the confrontation of two multiple-shaped worlds....The linguistic blend of these names signifies the superimpositions of heterogeneous cultural strands."[1] The words are the precipitates of the clash of disparate cultures—one with an alphabetic written language, many others without. They represent the attempt of the West to assimilate these other cultures into its own system of signs, either by translating foreign sounds into Western letters, or by rechristening the other culture altogether. And so, as they surface now upon the walls of Western museums, the names shiver with ambivalence. Are they pinned to the museum surface like dead things, objects of a victorious taxidermy, the conquests of the global expansion of the West? Or do they erupt within the museum as the return of the repressed, belying its old aspiration—to represent the achievements of a universal human culture—with haunting reminders of the multiplicity of cultures that the museum must erase? Floating, deracinated signs, liminal words now thrust upon the cultural center, Baumgarten's names are displaced objects, as much as instruments involved in the literal displacement of the people that they name.

Now, postmodernism celebrated the condition of displacement as perhaps its most important, defining characteristic, in opposition to the autonomous, placeless objects and yet centered subjectivity supposedly offered up by much modernist art (such as the floating mobiles of Alexander Calder, or the baseless, abstract pillars of Brancusi). At the moment of the emergence of Baumgarten's artistic projects in the late 1960s, nowhere was this transformed logic clearer than among those works now called "Earth" or "Land Art," whose practitioners increasingly forsook the spaces of gallery and culture for the wide, far off swaths of untouched nature. Eschewing modernist placelessness for often permanent marriages of art to its site, such work was however not only physically displaced from the cultural center, but also usually based its forms upon a new relationship to absence and displacement. Monumentalized in Michael Heizer's massive sculpture *Double Negative*—two identical sloping ramps dug into the ground on either side of a natural chasm—such a work of art offered an aesthetic experience where the viewer could gaze across an empty valley into an identical trough from which he or she was absent, a consequence of the more crucial and literal displacement of the viewer around a work without a center (the natural chasm, the literal hole at the work's heart).[2] Robert Smithson's similarly massive *Spiral Jetty* echoed this abyssal structure. Built in the mythic form of the spiral in a singularly inhospitable area of the Great Salt Lake, Smithson's sculpture could only be viewed in its entirety from above—say, in an airplane—while its physical apperception at the site offered up only a series of fragmentary views of the too-large whole, compelling the viewer to march again in circles, repetitively, around the absent center of the spiral itself. Importantly, in Earth Art, a new engagement with displacement seemed to entail that it would be the gap of nature around which the work of culture revolved.

We might see Lothar Baumgarten as the inheritor of such an understanding of both displacement and the new interplay between nature and culture entailed by the shift to postmodernism. However, Baumgarten's understanding of displacement does not remain abstract or aesthetic, a physical, spatial experience only. For its viewers, *AMERICA Invention* did of course entail an almost dizzying, vertiginous experience around an empty center; but Baumgarten's displacements were historical and temporal as much as spatial, calling attention to *real* displacements in the past as opposed to abstract experiences of the same. And Baumgarten's work explored the *real*—by which I mean social—as opposed to the purely aesthetic effects of a wide-ranging cultural decentering in the present. Baumgarten's first major solo exhibition in France, *Acces aux quais, tableaux Parisiens* (*Access to the Train Platforms,* 1985-86), traced such a decentering not in relation to Native American populations, but in terms of France's colonialist past. Creating an enlarged facsimile of a map of the number 9 line of the Parisian metro, Baumgarten replaced nearly all of the Napoleonic names of the individual stops ("Nation," "Republique") with other places and names ("Dien-Bien-Phu," "New Caledonia") or descriptive phrases ("total confusion," "Natural Man," "quiet racism," "unfounded optimism"), creating a new map of what had been an idealized, instrumentalized narrative of public space.

Despite these shifts, Baumgarten's earliest projects did take up a relationship to nature not unlike his American counterparts involved in Earth Art. They also took up a relationship to myth—man's earliest cultural negotiation of nature—as did the work of Robert Smithson. In Germany, Baumgarten had been a student of Joseph Beuys, after all, the great impresario in postwar European culture of a new engagement of art with myth and a new connection of art to nature and ecology. But Baumgarten's use of nature was never unmediated, involving instead fiction and manipulation; similarly his understanding of myth was not as a primary reserve of uncontaminated human nature, but as an already accomplished cultural displacement of what could be called natural. Thus, early works saw Baumgarten photographing in close-up an everyday variety of German kale or broccoli, and labeling it *Virgin Forest, Amazonas*, or painting over the same images with the names of South American indigenous peoples. Desire was being expressed here, not truth; dream, not fact; displacement, not discovery. Baumgarten would spend five years in the mid-1970s creating a film based on a Tupi myth entitled *The Origin of the Night*. Comprised of images of plants, animals, waterways, and forests, with textual captions giving us the name of objects usually of South American origin, the work was actually shot in the German forests of the Rhine.

Baumgarten's current proposal for *Watershed* returns to this early film. Now, as then, Baumgarten intends to explore a reasonably untouched area of a forest, not in a far off land, but in Beacon, New York, a wooded peninsula adjacent to the soon-to-be-opened satellite of the Dia Center for the Arts. This exploration, however, will not take a visual form. Since the 1980s, the increasing textual turn of Baumgarten's work paralleled a growing distrust of the links between traditional anthropological techniques and visual images. Instead, Baumgarten will produce a series of highly sensitive sound recordings to be stored on CD, a record of different noises characteristic of different times of the year in this area of Beacon: the sounds of the tides, of characteristic birds, of the toads that periodically enter the area to mate, as well as the differentiation of sounds at the site during the day as opposed to the night.

What should we make of these sounds? Like the proper names in Baumgarten's public inscriptions, here are noises recorded, preserved by the technical and scientific methods characteristic of Western modernity, ready for translation into a system of knowledge and interpretation. Of course, it remains to be seen what form the sounds will take in Baumgarten's final project. But the initial thrust of it reminds me of an old, childhood conundrum: If a tree falls in a forest without anyone there to hear it, does it make a sound? Is there, in other words, such a thing as a natural sound? Can a sound exist in isolation? Isn't sound already a human product, a first transformation and interpretation of the data of raw nature? Rather than natural, these sounds then would already be human, already cultural products.

As the sound recordings will preserve a moment in the history of an area soon to be transformed and potentially lost by the encroachment and increasing use of Beacon by the artistic community, we might see Baumgarten's proposal as acting out the other side of our childhood puzzle. We might take the proposal as a poetic doubling, a secondary elaboration, of the future fate of this area. The question then would not be does a tree falling in a forest make a sound if there is no one there to hear it. It might rather be: Does our entry into the woods imply the displacement of that which would have made the sounds? Or better: Does our presence imply

nature's absence? Even its destruction? We thus face, in Baumgarten's project, an evocation of impending loss. But the artist's larger deployment of displacement teaches a more far-reaching lesson. "Nature" is not something that we have lost, that we can lose; it is always that which has already been lost, it is the very model of the inaccessible. It is always displaced in the moment of man's attempts to experience it, to see it, to understand it—like a glass of water that spills every time you reach to grasp it. These are hard truths. There have been no virgin forests. No origins of night. Only dreams and desires of the same, only "polyphonic" signs, as Baumgarten might say, for us to navigate, between the Scylla and Charybdis of ambivalence and implication. No knowledge without displacement. No civilization without barbarism. No culture without destruction. ●

1. Lothar Baumgarten, "Sidetracks," *Galeries Magazine* (April/May 1990): 98.
2. See Rosalind Krauss' reading of this work in *Passages in Modern Sculpture* (Cambridge, MA: The MIT Press, 1977, 1981).

Lothar Baumgarten, Installation view of *Theatrum Botanicum*, 1995, Foundation Cartier, Paris, France.

Artist Project

Denning's Point State Park
Beacon

Lothar Baumgarten

Seven sound pieces
Seven rings for contemplation

Lothar Baumgarten's sculptures, photographs, and site-specific works focus on indigenous history, language, and culture. His 16mm film work includes *The Origin of the Night* (1977), filmed on the Rhine River, and *Aristocrats of the Jungle* (1980), filmed in Venezuela among the Yanōmami Indians. His books include *The Names of the Trees* (1982), *The Land of the Spotted Eagle* (1983), and *Carbon* (1990), a book of eleven short stories and 170 photographs reflecting upon life along the tracks of the United States railroad system.

Baumgarten's *Watershed* project will include a series of sculptural installations and an audio work for Denning's Point State Park. Denning's Point, a 67-acre peninsula along the Hudson River is a spectacular wildlife area and landscape of deciduous hardwoods adjacent to the Fishkill Creek estuary. Baumgarten's project will create small gathering places along the shoreline and woods of Denning's Point that will make this area accessible to neighborhood residents and visitors. Seven rings of different diameters will be placed selectively throughout the peninsula. They will function as a circle to sit in, or on, to watch and listen to the environmental sounds of wildlife—a location for contemplation. Baumgarten also plans to create audio recordings of seasonal atmospheric sounds collected from various species and habitats at Denning's Point including toads, insects, birds, rain, the river, ice, and fire. This audio recording will be produced as a set of compact discs that will be distributed locally and internationally.

Matthew Buckingham, *Definition*, 2000, 35mm slide projection with sound.

Matthew Buckingham

Janet Kraynak

The first thing one perceives in the film of Matthew Buckingham's *Amos Fortune Road* (1996) is the roaring sound of a car engine accompanied by a lengthy, traveling shot winding through the paths of a rambling, rural road. For several minutes, nothing else appears but this moving image as a car, in which the camera is placed, makes its way through a tunnel of trees against a symphony of creaking breaks and an accelerating engine. In the next shot, the car has stopped; a church steeple—architecturally locatable to somewhere in the Northeastern United States—is reflected in the rear view mirror, and the sound of birds chirping can be heard in the background. A text panel, like those from the era of silent movies, interrupts, telling us that it is August, and Sharon, the film's fictional protagonist, is spending her summer teaching children's theater in New Hampshire.

In these few, introductory scenes, Buckingham's approach to, and thinking behind, image-making emerge. In collapsing the eye of the mobile filming camera with that of the viewer, the artist situates the latter internal to the action rather than outside of it. The film's story unfolds in the viewer's lived present, carrying him/her along to participate in Sharon's journey, which becomes a search for clues to the mysteries of a road sign that bears the name Amos Fortune. Like Buckingham's other works, *Amos Fortune Road* is more than a film, straddling the line between film *and* sculptural installation. As such, his practice demonstrates a contemporary disregard for the boundaries of medium, merging the spatial and temporal domains in a single continuum. While all of his films could function as autonomous works, Buckingham presents each of them in carefully conceived environments. Film projectors and small speakers act as sculptural elements, photographs and drawings are mounted on the walls, and projections are aligned along the crevices of walls and floors, all functioning to shape the entire space. As a result, the viewer enters into the film/art work as opposed to standing apart from it.

At the same time, Buckingham reveals an acute self-consciousness about the representational past from which this contemporary tendency of

Matthew Buckingham, Two stills from the film *Amos Fortune Road*, 1996, 16mm black-and-white film.

merging media and disciplines emerge. Throughout his work, he deploys the techniques and trappings—and in some cases actual examples—from the history of film. His film installations utilize the now archaic 16mm reels, with their unmistakable whirring sounds; grainy, black-and-white images present a decidedly low-tech aesthetic, consciously undermining a fetishism for new technologies. Slide projections, color photographs, and audio complete the raw material of Buckingham's practice, which variously takes as its subjects: the myths and realities of the life of Abraham Lincoln (*The Truth About Lincoln*, 1992), the first dictionary of standard English (*Definition*, 2000), the history of (or rather ideology behind) physiognomy, (*Subcutaneous*, 2001), and, in collaboration with artist Joachim Koester, the anarchic community Christiania, founded in Copenhagen, Denmark, in 1971 (*Sandra of the Tuliphouse or How to Live in a Free State*, 2001). What binds Buckingham's many projects together is a defining of the present through the model of the flashback—an endless loop of recurrences—that produces a commentary on the nature of art objects and historical understanding as well.

Amos Fortune Road centers on Sharon's discovery of a historical marker on the side of a busy intersection that she passes each day while driving to class with one of her students, Maryanne. This encounter provides the catalyst for a complex dance in which historical fact and mythology are investigated through the actual figure of Amos Fortune, a slave who purchased his freedom in 1769 and went on to help found a local public library. During the course of the film, various questions arise as to the identity of Amos Fortune: what the local community knows, and how or whether or not his history, and by association that of African Americans, has entered into official "American" history. Weaving together the film's various threads is the seemingly unending drive, which both visually frames and ultimately becomes the primary content of the piece—the experience of traveling on these roads provides the sole access to Amos Fortune, whose path to emancipation from Massachusetts to New Hampshire followed their same trajectory. At the center of Sharon's quest—and by extension Buckingham's film—is thus the literal and figurative absence of Amos Fortune, who remains largely unknown despite diligent research.

The repetitive shots of driving in *Amos Fortune Road* has led some critics to describe it in terms of the genre of the road movie. But viewing it brought to my mind the artist Tony Smith's now famous description of surreptitiously driving on the unfinished New Jersey Turnpike in the early sixties. A blighted landscape of small hills, abandoned industrial structures, and distant lights unfolded as Smith made his way down the turnpike, which, unfinished, existed in a liminal state between road and non-road: paved but bearing no markers or shoulders. The experience prompted Smith to reflect upon—or rather to come to a realization of—the limitations of the conventional nature of art objects. "The road and much of the landscape was artificial," he recalled, "and yet it couldn't be called a work of art. On the other hand, it did something for me that art had never done... It seemed there was a reality there which had not had any expression in art." In Smith's mind, the drive on the turnpike became an art work—but one which emerged by virtue of his encounter with it, suggesting a critical shift in what constitutes an art "object" and how it produces meaning. In other words, rather than a thing made, subsequently presented for viewing, its existence was dependent upon a type of performance to bring it into being. "There is no way you can frame it," he continued, "you just have to experience it."

Buckingham's work emerges from this legacy, as his art objects—conceived as spatialized films—do not simply relay a story or convey meaning, but create situations to be experienced. Thematically, the story of *Amos Fortune Road*, like Smith's foray onto the turnpike, is the product of an encounter: the one Sharon experiences, which, it could be surmised, replicates that of the artist. Similarly, in a more recent piece, *Situation Leading to a Story*, the artist's discovery of a box of discarded home movies on a New York City street becomes the basis for an art work *cum* investigation. Two adjoining rooms comprise the installation: the first one containing the film projector that projects the images through a small hole in the wall into the second space. The films, on weathered black-and-white film (which, Buckingham uncovers, dates from the twenties and thirties), present four different stories: a garden party, the building of a cable tramway at a copper mine in Peru, the construction of a garage addition at the private home where the first film was made, and a bullfight in Guadalajara. Buckingham embarks upon a fact-finding mission—recounted in a voice-over juxtaposed against the four films—to discover the possible connection between them, who the owner was, and why they were tossed into the garbage bin.

The casting-off of the aging films in *Situation* and the continual oscillation between the present tense of Buckingham's narrative voice and the past tense of the imagery, emerges as a metaphor for our relationship to the past—a theme that continually enters into Buckingham's projects. Part anthropology, part cultural history, *Situation* and *Amos Fortune Road* aim to exceed the bounds of art/aesthetics altogether in order to say something about a larger subject: namely, historical or cultural knowledge. History, like the conventional notion of art objects, is popular-

Matthew Buckingham, Installation view of *Situation Leading to a Story*, 1999, 16mm black-and-white film,
PS1 Contemporary Art Center.

Matthew Buckingham, Six stills from *Situation Leading to a Story*, 1999, 16mm black-and-white film.

"Part anthropology, part cultural history, *Situation* and *Amos Fortune Road* aim to exceed the bounds of art/aesthetics altogether in order to say something about a larger subject: namely, historical or cultural knowledge. History, like the conventional notion of art objects, is popularly understood to be an ossified thing whose temporality is in the past. It is about completion and our relationship to it is one of passive reception. But for Buckingham, history is restless, subject to flux. Figured as participants in, rather than omniscient witnesses of, the mysteries of *Amos Fortune Road* and *Situation* (which, incidentally, are never fully resolved) the viewers engage in the creation of the work and, by association, history itself."

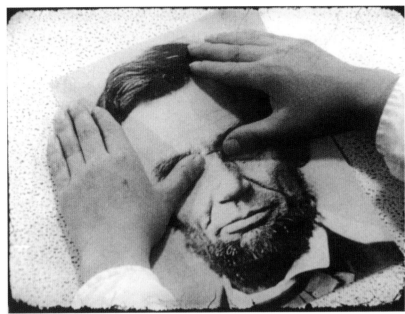

Matthew Buckingham, *The Truth About Lincoln*, 1992, 16mm black and white film.

ly understood to be an ossified thing whose temporality is in the past. It is about completion and our relationship to it is one of passive reception. But for Buckingham, history is restless, subject to flux. Figured as participants in, rather than omniscient witnesses of, the mysteries of *Amos Fortune Road* and *Situation* (which, incidentally, are never fully resolved), the viewers engage in the creation of the work and, by association, history itself.

The filmic genres upon which Buckingham draws—including "serious" documentary, travelogue, and home movies, to name a few—are specifically deployed in this project. Their shared image conventions—for example, black-and-white pictures, a limited use of obvious, manipulated camera work, and a dispassionate voice of an unseen narrator—intend to suggest objectivity and an allegiance to truth, despite constituting, in actuality, aesthetic choices. In Buckingham's work, analogies are created between these cinematic and photographic modes and historical knowledge: both sharing a similar pretense to what the French philosopher, Roland Barthes, describes as the *reality-effect*. While employing such signs of the real and truth, however, Buckingham carefully undermines their legitimacy. This is achieved through the frustrating of narrative closure at the heart of his films (i.e., we never learn the identity of the "real" Amos Fortune, nor the relations between the discarded films of *Situation*, nor the truth of Abe Lincoln's legacy). The ultimate unknowability of the stories that comprise his films operate as an analogue for the very inaccessibility of historical truth, which, Buckingham suggests, is subject to the manipulations of time and vagaries of image making. As a result, what we are left with is that history is not something that can be documented or "framed," but, like Sharon comes to realize in *Amos Fortune Road*, must be passed through and continually experienced. •

Artist Project   Venues throughout the Hudson Valley

Matthew Buckingham

Muhheakantuck—
Everything has a Name

The European-American history of the Hudson is just a moment in the great sweep of geological and native time in the Hudson Valley.... If European explorers laid claim to the lands of the New World by the act of naming, then we must recognize the prior claim of native peoples inherent in [the indigenous name for the river] "Muhheakantuck" and examine the disposition of that claim by the Europeans.

Matthew Buckingham's site-specific works include films, videos, drawings, and sculptures that probe the untold stories of cultural personages and their lives and communities. His recent film and installation works include *The Truth About Abraham Lincoln*, *Situation Leading to a Story*, and *Amos Fortune Road*.

Buckingham's *Watershed* project *Muhheakantuck — Everything Has a Name* will examine issues of history and cartography in relationship to the Hudson River. As part of this work, Buckingham will assemble a small group of historians and geographers of the Hudson Valley to advise and contribute to his research. The resulting project is comprised of a film installation, a map project, and a symposium organized in collaboration with one of the five colleges and universities participating in *Watershed*.

West Side Heliport, Manhattan

West side of Manhattan,
Hudson River and New Jersey

Indian Point Nuclear Power Plant,
Peekskill, New York

Franklin D. Roosevelt's bedroom
with telephone hot-line to White
House, Hyde Park, New York

New Hamburg, New York

Nyack, New York

Beacon, New York

East bank of the Hudson River
at Greystone, New York

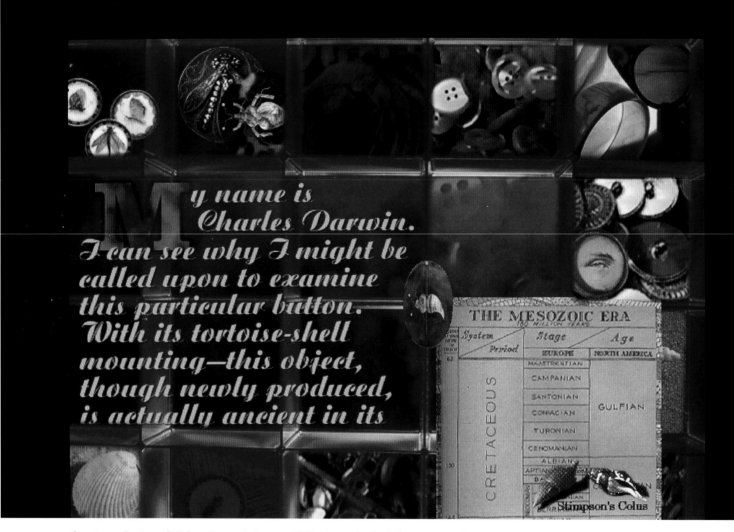

Constance De Jong, Still from *Fantastic Prayers*, 2000, Interactive CD-ROM, courtesy of Dia Center for the Arts (a collaboration with Tony Oursler and Stephen Vitiello).

Constance De Jong

Carlo McCormick

There is a place—off the page, off the tongue, amidst people, and always somewhat apart from what it is supposed to describe—where language exists at some impalpable and intangible interstice of memory and the mind. In an extensive oeuvre that spans a quarter of a century, Constance De Jong hasn't really ever articulated this space, she's simply created it. De Jong eschews the formal constraints of narrative for a sublime sonic poetics that is less linear than purely linguistic. Her discretion of representation and obviation of typical, vernacular story-telling, however, does not simply lead to the rapture of words. Like the work of the best composers, De Jong's words are neither accidental nor incidental but finely crafted and detailingly worked strophes that build in cumulative effect towards the mesmeric state of open-ended suggestibility. Written and spoken, De Jong conjures her pictures as something we must hear to see. Hers is a kind of imagistic, meditative text that never declaims the truth so much as invokes its mystery. Although cerebral in its construction, what this author ultimately has to tell us is bound to the fragile emotive topography and deeply introspective space of the human psyche. So just try to forget about the legacy of literature for a change. If you want to understand De Jong's work, you must first realize that it's not something to be analyzed or explained. First, you have to listen.

If it is the sound of language and its compelling capacity to evoke specific images in the mind's eye of each individual that is the medium for De Jong's performative communication process, then its improbable physicality is something like a wave. This wave, most literally the oscillation of tone itself, is perhaps many other things as well. Sound becomes a phenomenological vehicle or a temporal bridge to span the perceptual chasm between the page and the mind. As an author, De Jong finds her precedents in writers like Gertrude Stein, Virginia Wolf, and Marguerite Duras. But it is as an artist, who has consistently resisted the temptation of allowing the page to be the final repository of her ideas, that De Jong has leaped across the spectrum of multimedia.

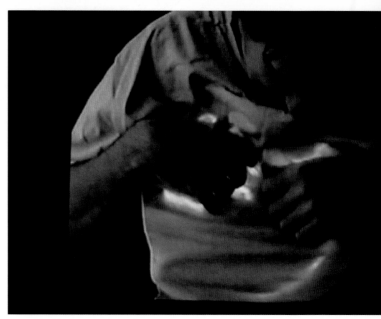

Constance De Jong, *Scry Agency*, 2001, multimedia performance,
Thread Waxing Space, New York City.

"…it is as an artist, who has consistently resisted the temptation of allowing the page to be the final repository of her ideas, that De Jong has leaped across the spectrum of multimedia."

Arriving in New York City in the mid-1970's, De Jong immersed herself in the germinal SoHo loft performance scene. There, the radical artistic experiments conducted within austere formal constructs—such as the performance art of Meredith Monk and Yvonne Rainer, the modern dance of Tricia Brown, avant-garde films of Michael Snow, and the musical compositions of Philip Glass (with whom De Jong would collaborate on subsequent projects)—informed her about the expanding possibilities of new genres, as well as how an artist's investment in his/her work did not end with its "completion" but extended to its projection out into the world. By the time De Jong produced her first substantial textual work, *Modern Love*, in 1975, she was already wary of settling into the passive form of the novel. Over a course of nearly two years, *Modern Love* was adopted into myriad forms, starting out serialized through six different books posted to friends in the art world as mail art, becoming the material for her first public reading at the Kitchen, and then morphing into a radio program with accompanying music by Philip Glass. This kind of fluidity through the bounds of medium, both an irascibility towards such constraints and a pragmatic way of navigating from the solitude of a writer's life into the social discourse of the world at large, is as endemic to De Jong's earliest work as it is to her recent projects.

De Jong's longstanding interest in transcending the limits of pure text has also brought her into collaboration with prominent artists from other disciplines. Her libretto for Philip Glass' *Satyagraha*, an opera spectacle based on the life of Ghandi, as well as her extended body of work with video installation artist Tony Oursler, including *Fantastic Prayers*, which evolved from a live event to an epic CD-ROM of elaborate architecture over a period of more than five years, attest to De Jong's willingness to weave language into more musical and visual realms, stretching her vision across diverse forms of expression. In a similar vein, her "talking benches" along the Hudson River in Battery Park City or the Thames River along the Canary Wharf in London (2000), move far beyond literature, performance art, and spoken word. Part sculpture, public art, and sound installation, this project, entitled *Speaking of the River*, demonstrates just how far she has journeyed from the word itself and how fully integrated her hybrid meta-text is with the visual

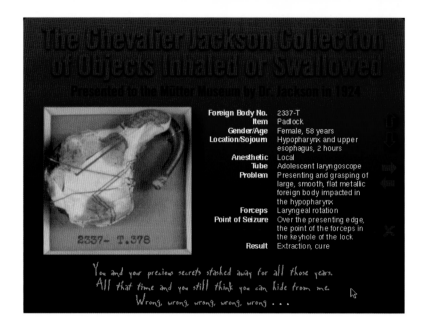

The Chevalier Jackson Collection
of Objects Inhaled or Swallowed

Presented to the Mütter Museum by Dr. Jackson in 1924

Foreign Body No.	2337-T
Item	Padlock
Gender/Age	Female, 58 years
Location/Sojourn	Hypopharynx and upper esophagus, 2 hours
Anesthetic	Local
Tube	Adolescent laryngoscope
Problem	Presenting and grasping of large, smooth, flat metallic foreign body impacted in the hypopharynx
Forceps	Laryngeal rotation
Point of Seizure	Over the presenting edge, the point of the forceps in the keyhole of the lock
Result	Extraction, cure

2337- T.378

*You and your precious secrets stashed away for all those years.
All that time and you still think you can hide from me.
Wrong, wrong, wrong, wrong, wrong . . .*

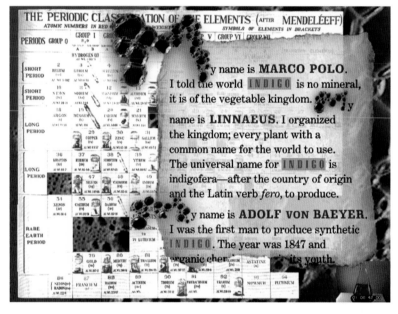

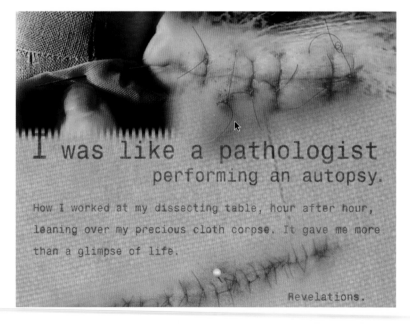

terms of contemporary art. Specifically, this artist has taken a very conscious and conceptually precise position in regards to the conjunction of imagery and text. De Jong is interested in the accumulation and layering of information. The visual is never an illustration of the story. Rather, via her increasing use of digital technologies, De Jong fabricates new forms for stories and pictures to inhabit the same space.

De Jong uses technology as a pragmatic delivery system for her ideas. As with her benches, and their recent forerunner in her *Duets for Animals and People* at the Seattle Zoo, De Jong's talking objects rely on the relative simplicity of voice chips and sensors to conjure the magic of animated objects that talk to us. Compared to much of contemporary digital art in which technology becomes a toy that overdetermines the work, De Jong takes what she needs of the intelligent machines in the most organic service of her aesthetic intentions. Spawned perhaps from her first collaborations with Oursler in the early 1980's, single-channel videos integrating pictures and words, De Jong's recent talking objects (such as her multiple, *Writer's Block*, a tabletop steel cube) continue to converge the visual and linguistic as integral rather than supplemental processes. Perhaps the more intangible connection between De Jong's art and technology, however, is the peculiar process of memory as it retains and wields sums of information.

De Jong has a facility to relate lengthy literary tracts by memory. More than a tremendous performance skill, her memory allows her to hold elaborate non-linear constructs in the shape of narrative, like some elaborate edifice that can maintain its baroque architecture, while she continues to work from within it and build upon it. And, in the same way that silicone chips facilitate rapid access of vast amounts of pre-stored data, De Jong is concerned with the role of memory as a dimension of the present tense, as the non-specific moment that connects the work with its viewer/reader. She has never wanted to read her work aloud, believing the page is dead, a relic of the past. Rather, her interest in memory as a way of putting her words in the present is bound to an understanding that language occurs phenomenologically in real time. In her *Speaking of the River* benches, whispering to us the secrets of the river, its past, and the many lives of long ago that now haunt it, memory unfolds as if carried by the currents of nature's most potent symbol for return and the continuous cycles of existence. And what we hear is something beyond the sound of the writer's voice, or the imprints of language upon an encoding system. They are the hushed transitory messages of time itself, the sounds of a society of souls that is the living history of the ever flowing discourse between humanity and nature. ●

99

OPPOSITE Constance De Jong, Still from *Fantastic Prayers*, 2000, Interactive CD-ROM, courtesy of Dia Center for the Arts (a collaboration with Tony Oursler and Stephen Vitiello).

Speaking of the River

View of Madam Brett Park

Constance De Jong is a writer and performance artist who has worked collaboratively with composers and video artists on multidisciplinary works, performances, and public projects. Past works include *Relatives* and *Fantastic Prayers*, performance collaborations with Tony Oursler; and *Satyagraha*, an opera with Phillip Glass.

De Jong's *Speaking of the River* is an audio work for sound-equipped benches at Madam Brett Park, at the mouth of Fishkill Creek and adjacent to the Beacon Terminal buildings in Beacon. Formerly a grist mill and cotton factory, Beacon Terminal is best known as the site of the Tioronda Hat Works, one of the many hat and textile manufacturing buildings in Beacon at the turn of the century. For her project, *Speaking of the River*, Constance De Jong will interview former mill workers, current residents, and recent immigrants to Beacon, whose stories will form the spoken text of *Speaking of the River*. These customized benches are fitted with a proximity sensor in the armrest. When seated, a person interrupts this sensor and initiates the sound system that plays the recorded material. Approximately ten texts will comprise the final recording. This work will also be produced as a compact disc, which will be available in locations throughout Beacon and distributed internationally. This project will be developed with Scenic Hudson, the City of Beacon, and neighborhood residents in Beacon.

Constance De Jong, *Portrait (unfinished)*, 1985, Joan Logue.

View of Bear Mountain State Park

ABOVE Peter Hutton, Still from film, *Study of a River*, 1997.

BELOW Peter Hutton, Still from film, *Time and Tide*, 2001.

Peter Hutton

Scott MacDonald

Art historian Barbara Novak's famous distinction between two approaches to the American landscape in nineteenth-century painting—"grand opera" "and the still small voice"—remains useful for twentieth-century film. To a significant degree, the grand landscape epitomized by Frederic Edwin Church and "The Rocky Mountain School" (Albert Bierstadt, Thomas Moran, Thomas Hill) became, and remains, the literal and historical background of epic commercial films, from the earliest attempts to interest filmgoers in natural scenes, to John Ford's *Stagecoach* (1939), *Fort Apache* (1948), and *The Searchers* (1956), to more recent hits like *Dances With Wolves* (1990) and *Legends of the Fall* (1995). This "grand opera" sensibility has also played a major role in the history of independent feature filmmaking, from Robert Flaherty's *Nanook of the North* (1921) to Godfrey Reggio's *Koyaanisqatsi* (1984) and Robert Fricke's *Baraka* (1993). But the "still small voice" also seems alive, not as a major influence on commercial cinema but as a sensibility of considerable importance in coming to terms with a number of landmark American independent films of recent decades. The films of Peter Hutton are a case in point.

During the thirty-plus years of his career as an independent filmmaker, Hutton has demonstrated a remarkably consistent aesthetic in a series of motion pictures that confront conventional assumptions about what cinema can and should do. As Hutton himself has explained: "Most people go to films to get some kind of hit, some kind of overwhelming experience, whether it's like an amusement park ride or an ideological, informational hit that gives you a critical insight into an issue or an idea. But for those people who feel they need a reprieve occasionally, who want to cleanse the palate a bit, whether for spiritual or physiological reasons, these films seem to be somewhat effective."[1] Hutton has consistently used minimal means with maximum dexterity to provide an experience of film-going that is simultaneously distinctive and deeply referential to the histories of film, still photography, and painting. And while it is true that few people have found their way to Hutton's work (compared to mass audiences for commercial films), this has less to do with the potential of these films to please audiences than with the general cultural marginalization of avant-garde cinema in America. In fact, more and more filmgoers are finding the "reprieve" Hutton offers not only accessible and enjoyable, but transformative.

Hutton's minimal means—his commitment to black-and-white, silent imagery, shot with a 16mm camera mounted on a tripod, and presented as a series of extended, discrete views—represent a conscious return to the earliest cinema, and in particular to the Lumière Brothers and their use of the Cinématographe to produce single-shot movies, photographs-in-motion, that could reveal both familiar surroundings and exotic locales in new, entertaining ways. For Hutton, the Lumières are important not so much for the popular cinema their camera and public presentations helped to inspire, but for what their simple approach has to offer us *now*. Hutton extends the Lumières' approach into new visual territory, so that viewers can discover a new way of thinking about film and film-going.

Generally speaking, Hutton has focused on two topics: cityscape and landscape. He has made a series of "portraits" of New York City (where he lived, off and on, from 1972 until 1985, in between working as a merchant seaman in Thailand, and teaching and filmmaking jobs at Hampshire College, Harvard, and in Berlin): *New York, Near Sleep (for Saskia)* (1972), *New York Portrait, Part I* (1979), *Part II* (1981), *Part III* (1990). He has also traveled to other cities to make portraits there: to Budapest (*Budapest Portrait [Memory of a City]*, 1986) and Lodz, Poland (*Lodz Symphony*, 1993). The results are highly unusual city films,

nearly the inversion of the City Symphony form that originated in Europe in the 1920's with *Berlin: Symphony of a Big City* (1927, directed by Walther Ruttmann) and *The Man with a Movie Camera* (1929, by Dziga Vertov). The City Symphony sings the energy of the modern city and the excitement and power of modern industrialization as it has developed in the quintessential urban centers of modern nation states. Hutton's city portraits, in contrast, discover the quiet spaces and intimate moments of city life, and ask that we consider cities not simply as places where high concentrations of people and industry create unusual intensity, but as environments that provide a wide range of possibilities, including spaces/moments for contemplation and meditation.

In 1985 Hutton was appointed Assistant Professor of Film at Bard College, and moved to Annandale-on-Hudson with his family (Hutton married composer Margaret De Wys in 1992; they have one daughter, Manon). Hutton has taught there ever since, and in recent years has chaired Bard's Department of Film and Electronic Arts. Bard's location on the Hudson River within sight of the Catskill Mountains has not been lost on Hutton, who has produced a series of landscape films that evoke the considerable tradition of depicting the Hudson Valley, and in particular, the Hudson River School of American landscape painting.

The first of these films, *Landscape (for Manon)* (1987), is one of Hutton's most impressive. In twenty-two shots, Hutton presents the landscape in the area of Kaaterskill Clove, the valley created by Kaaterskill Creek that was the subject of so many paintings by Thomas Cole and

"Hutton's serene, evocative landscapes are, in this instance, qualified by an environmental problem—one that confronts our hunger for imagery of pristine nature."

the painters his work inspired. With two exceptions each shot is separated from the next by a fade-out, a moment of darkness, and a fade-in (shots 3 and 4, and 15 and 16, are dyads); and, in a strategy that reverses the tendency of most films to accelerate as the action develops, Hutton's landscape film begins with extended shots (the first four shots last for twenty-five, twenty-seven, eleven, and twenty-seven seconds, respectively) and then *slows down* (midway through *Landscape [for Manon]* the individual shots last more than forty seconds). The length of Hutton's black-and-white, silent shots creates an unusual experience for viewers, especially since, at first, almost nothing seems to be happening in some of the individual images: viewers may wonder if some of the images are still photographs. As the seconds pass, however, even the least active of Hutton's images subtly evolve, and viewers realize that the entire scene is shifting, transforming the shape and chiaroscuro of the image, and revealing that each Hutton image is not only *not* still, but is a microcosm of much larger orders of motion that dwarf the limited rectangular world defined by the film frame. The closing shot of *Landscape (for Manon)*—a superimposition of the child, Manon, sleeping and mot-

tled shadows made by sunlight shining through leaves—suggests not only Hutton's affection for his daughter and, perhaps, his belief that children may find it easier to access the beauties of the natural world than busy, distracted adults, but also that his film is a gift to those filmgoers-as-sleeping-children who need to be reconnected to a primary perceptual experience of the world around them.

In 1991 Hutton followed his first Hudson Valley landscape film with *In Titan's Goblet*, named for Thomas Cole's *The Titan's Goblet* (1833), that anomalous, small painting in which a giant goblet is set within a mountainous landscape. Like *Landscape (for Manon)*, *In Titan's Goblet* depicts in a series of often-stunning, silent, black-and-white, discrete images the Catskill Mountain area. In this case, however, a sequence of lovely images of what at first appears to be mist in the mountains is slowly revealed to be a distant fire of rubber tires that had burned out of control. That is, Hutton's serene, evocative landscapes are, in this instance, qualified by an environmental problem—one that confronts our hunger for imagery of pristine nature. This more double-sided envisioning is also evident in the two most recent films Hutton has made in the Hudson Valley: *Study of a River*

Peter Hutton, Still from film, *Time and Tide*, 2001.

(1997) and *Time and Tide* (2000), the first two parts of what Hutton expects to be an extended, multipartite film on the Hudson River.

Like Hutton's earlier films, *Study of a River* is a black-and-white, silent study, in this case, of the Hudson in winter, focusing to a large extent on the shipping traffic that moves up and down the river, year round, filmed sometimes from boats on the river and at others from the riverbank or from an old railroad bridge that spans the Hudson at Poughkeepsie. *Time and Tide* expands the stunning vision of *Study of a River* in several ways. First, *Time and Tide* begins with a short film produced in 1903 by the American Mutoscope and Biograph Company: *Down the Hudson*, which in fact depicts a voyage *up* the Hudson—from Haverstraw through the Hudson Highlands to Newburg—at hyper-speed, by using time-lapse shooting. Hutton's recycling of this early film connects his film with the history of cinematic depictions of the Hudson *and* it creates a particularly dramatic context for what follows: Hutton's typically serene evocation of the river in long, continuous shots made from various boats and barges voyaging up and down the river.

Time and Tide is also Hutton's first film to use color, as well as black and white (Hutton has shot color in his work as cinematographer on projects produced by others, including his former student, documentarian, Ken Burns), and it is, at thirty-five minutes, Hutton's longest film to date. That Hutton would expand his means for *this* subject suggests how crucial the Hudson has become for him, both as an evocation of America's and his own years as a merchant seaman, and as a threatened environment: *Time and Tide* presents beautiful imagery of the Hudson *and* regularly evokes several, current environmental controversies having to do with cleaning up the river.

As the new millennium gets underway, Peter Hutton is making some of his finest films and continues to expand the range of his cinematic explorations. As this is written, Hutton is finishing *Looking at the Sea*, shot on the west coast of Ireland and on the Island of Aran, and shooting footage on the Yangtze River and in the Guilin region of China. •

1. Interview with the author, in Scott MacDonald, *A Critical Cinema* (Berkeley: University of California Press, 1999), 243.

Peter Hutton

Two Rivers

Peter Hutton, Still from 16mm black-and-white film, *Study of a River*, 1997.

From 1988 until 1997, filmmaker Peter Hutton completed a four-part filmic study of the Hudson River entitled *Study of a River*. His recent films also include *Landscape*, *New York Portrait*, *Lodz Symphony*, and *Budapest Portrait*.

Peter Hutton's *Watershed* project, *Two Rivers*, is inspired by the third voyage of Henry Hudson in his quest for the trade route to the Great China Sea in 1609, and J.M.W. Turner's painting, *Snowstorm — Steamboat off harbour's mouth making signals in shallow water and going by the lead* (circa 1842). As part of this project, Hutton will film the Three Gorges area of the Yangtze River in China, the Arctic Sea, and the Hudson River from the Adirondacks to the Battery. This work will include a film installation in commercial venues such as outdoor film theaters, and non-traditional venues such as abandoned mill buildings and quarries.

OPPOSITE Peter Hutton, Still from 16mm black-and-white film, *Study of a River*, 1997.

Claude Lorrain Glasses, from the eighteenth century.

Matts Leiderstam

Gertrud Sandqvist

Matts Leiderstam's art has as much to do with observation as with creation. Again and again, he rearranges the relationship between the artist and the viewer: sometimes he forces the viewer to abandon his/her disinterested position to contribute to the creative process, other times he abandons the creative imperative of the artist himself to assume the perspective of the viewer. In this regard, Leiderstam's work is in line with Marcel Duchamp's investigations, constantly constructing and dismantling our expectations in a game in which the poles of activity and passivity shift continuously. The fact that Leiderstam's artistic investigations also involve his own and the viewer's sexuality further underlines the Duchamp connection. But unlike Duchamp, and subsequently a number of other avant-garde artists, Leiderstam has not turned away from painting. In fact, painting and its priority of vision provide him with an opportunity to engage aspects of art that deal with the production of desire.

Given his interest in painting and the production of desire, and given that art collecting is one of the most obvious manifestations of the fetishism of art, it is perhaps no surprise that Leiderstam also takes an interest in the phenomenon of art collecting, both personal and institutional. In numerous projects Leiderstam has been preoccupied with the issue of how museum collections can be understood not only in terms of historical and formal criteria but as results of meetings, wishes, and desires. In the museum, perhaps more than anywhere else, the artist and the viewer meet, sometimes changing roles in relation to the art work.

Leiderstam also maintains an ongoing interest in the park and its functions, particularly as a "secret" place for encounters between gay men. Whether Central Park in New York or Frescati in Stockholm, parks accommodate different uses and have multiple connotations depending on the identity and predilection of the user. In a series of pointillist paintings from the early 1990s, Leiderstam renders scenes of an idyllic family park that happen to include nocturnal gay cruising areas, forming a double perspective which he has developed in a number of other works.[1] For

Matts Leiderstam, *View*, Scaniaplatsen, Västra Hamnen, Malmö 2001.

Leiderstam, the cruising culture's anonymous sexual encounters in parks find a counterpart in the museum—both sites being a *locus classicus* for casual (imagined) erotic encounters. In other words, the museum is a place for "cruising," too, where one can view and interact with painted and sculpted bodies as well as the bodies of other visitors. Whether intense or causal, such meetings—between gay men in parks, or between art and its viewer in museums— are anonymous and the partings are discrete, without deep emotional complications or abiding obligations. There is a similar matter-of-factness or liberty to the practice of cruising and the act of viewing art in museums.

Since 1996, Leiderstam has done much work in relation to a painting by Nicolas Poussin entitled *Spring* or *The Earthly Paradise* from *The Four Seasons* suite (1660-1664). It depicts Adam and Eve in an Arcadian landscape, just before the Fall, with God departing the scene on a cloud. One reason for Leiderstam's fascination with this painting is that it served as a model for the development of the English garden and park in the seventeenth and eighteenth centuries. In addition, the painting is an ideal picture of "cruisable" grounds; it depicts a mysterious dark area to the left (a cave?) that resonates with "dark holes" in cruising parks, such as the darkness provided by shrubbery or a small grove, into which

Matts Leiderstam, *View*, Scaniaplatsen, Malmo, 2001.

one can disappear. Visually, too, the dark area of *Spring* or *The Earthly Paradise*, like the discrete yet persistent dark corners in all of Poussin's landscapes, marks a point where the viewer's eyes can "fall."[2]

Leiderstam has developed two different projects engaging this particular Poussin painting. In *Cruising with Nicolas Poussin* (1996) and a series entitled *Returned* (1997-2001),[3] Leiderstam painted copies of *Spring* or *The Earthly Paradise*, but removed Adam, Eve, and God, depicting only the landscape. The copies were then exhibited to the public in eccentric ways. *Cruising* was displayed on the floor, placed in such a way so that the visitor may consciously or inadvertently walk on it. The paint from their shoes was then dispersed throughout the rest of the exhibition space as the visitors traced their own passage in the act of walking and viewing art. In the *Returned* series, Leiderstam's copies of Poussin's painting, resting on an easel, were placed at specific spots in various well-known parks that also function as cruising areas (the artist found the spots following *The Spartacus Gay Guide)*. He then pho-

tographed his copies in situ, in the park landscape of smooth and pleasant nature. Once photographed, the paintings were abandoned there; the audience of the *Returned* series can only view these photographs of the painting as it was left on the easel.

First, the act of manually copying an "original" work, which used to be the sole means of reproducing a painting and a compulsory part of an artist's training, is today only practiced by amateurs and considered a rather lowly endeavor. But for Leiderstam, the etymological root of the word "amateur," linked to the lover (Lat. *amator*, from *amare*, to love) and the shifting value associated with copying—from skilled work to passionate engagement—opens up an ambiguous area for further exploration of sexuality and vision.

In a number of other works, Leiderstam varies his relation to the museum and the copy. *The Eruption of Vesuvius* (2000) is a photographic triptych involving a 1771 painting of the same title by Pierre-Jacques-Antoine Volaire,[4] which is part of the Art Institute of Chicago collection. In one of the photographs of the triptych, we see Leiderstam's copy "returned" to the edge of Mount Vesuvius. The two other photographs show Volaire's original as it hung in the home of an affluent family in Gothenburg, Sweden, during the 1940s, and its current display at the Art Institute of Chicago. Here, through Leiderstam's framing of the photograph—in which Volaire's "eruption" is flanked by a Hubert Robert painting of an obelisk seen through an arch, and a painting of Aries, the god of war, passionately embracing Aphrodite—the overly (hetero)sexualized curatorial vision becomes explicit. In works like *The Eruption of Vesuvius*, Leiderstam makes it impossible to think of meaning as something divorced from historical or physical contexts. At the same time, he questions the difference that is normally attributed to the home and the museum as sites of artistic appreciation.

Yet in other works, Leiderstam draws the viewer's attention to the power of the gaze and the secret homoerotic game that is concealed and revealed in certain paintings. This is the case in *Blue Vision* (1998), a video installation piece that establishes a complex interplay between *Portrait of a Young Man* by Bernardino Licinio da Pordenone (early sixteenth century), *Boy Playing Flute* by Frans Hals (1645-1650), and *Gentleman* by Jan de Brey (after 1670). In an e-mail exchange with Friedemann Malsch, the director of the Kunstmuseum Liechtenstein, Leiderstam writes about his first encounter with the portrait by da Pordenone:

> When I first saw the painting in your storage room, it looked like a young man who did not reveal much, but at the same time gave me a promising look: a gaze of recognition that I know from gay cruising. His mouth was—I write "was" since the painting has become something different after its restoration—curved in a slightly amused expression. This, together with the look in his eyes, told me that he might be aware of the fact that he is the object for someone else's desire and that he may have enjoyed it. I can also draw a parallel between this interpretation and a vague, distant memory of myself at the same age: when a man—or a woman—looked at me as I am now looking at the portrait. I could not deal with this kind of gaze then, while at the same time I felt excited and flattered by it, but I was frightened. The portrait brings me back to the same kind of situation, making me into an object.[5]

Leiderstam describes here an intricate play of desires and gazes, between his own, as a viewer, and those of the young man of the painting, simultaneously objectifying the young man (like da Pordenone did?) and imagining or remembering himself objectified by other's gazes.

The issue of likeness and doubling extend into more recent projects. While preparing for *Blue Vision*, Leiderstam discovered that the portrait had changed from the first time he saw it. It had been "restored," and the transformation was astonishing. This metamorphosis of the painting served as the key point of *Before and After* (1999), in which photographs of the unrestored and restored portrait were exhibited side by side. In *Adolf Ludvig Stierneld* (2000) and *He and She*

(2001), Leiderstamd similarly paired two photographs of paintings without frames and "returned" to the easel. The first shows two eighteenth-century portraits of the same man, painted by two different artists, one male and one female. Whereas Ulrika Pasch saw a virile and seductive man, Jacob Björk, or his copyist, saw a rather vulgar and effeminate one. The second, *He and She*, shows Isak Wacklin's 1755 portraits of a married couple—Reverend Samuel Wacklin and his wife Elisabeth in Laihela—in which the contracting parties look so much alike that they could be taken for twins. (Moreover, the artist is the brother of the portrayed man.) In all these works, the Leiderstam is interested in the issue of likeness, albeit not in the usual sense. His playful game with artists, models, paintings, and viewers remind us of the fundamental instability of these roles.

Generally, Leiderstam reveals our need to see and to be seen, although to admit to such a need is to reveal one's vulnerability. I associate his rambles in parks and museums with the loneliness and longing that is tied to this need and vulnerability, aspects of our being too often hidden or repressed from view in professional contexts as signs of amateurism. However, when Leiderstam voluntarily takes on the role of the amateur/copyist in major museum collections, he also assumes the role of the lover, changing the stakes and questioning the rules of the game. He reorganizes the pieces so as to make us, his audience, less certain. He entices—or forces—the viewer to act, to give up our comfortable passivity in relation to the artist and the art work. By rocking his own position to its foundations, he dares the viewer to take risks, too. ●

1. *Tableau* (1990-1992), an installation of four paintings, includes *Morning*, *Noon*, *Evening*, and *Night*.

2. In the catalogue for the 1996 group exhibition "See What It Feels Like" at Rooseum in Malmö, Sweden, Margaretha Rossholm-*Lagerlöf* writes: "All of Poussins landscape paintings have at the center of the foreground a dark surface, located in a corner, usually to the left—a surface which may be interpreted as vegetation or some dark rocks. To me, these surfaces at the 'entrance' of the world of the image, are a passage which the eye must follow, a descent border to cross. After that, you enter a pictorial world of magical force, present in all its physical fragility."

3. The works that are part of the *Returned* series are *Returned, Hempstead Heath* (London, 1997), *Returned, The Rambles* (Central Park, New York, 1997), *Returned, Parc Mont Royal* (Montréal, 1998), *Returned, Park K. Marcinkowskiego* (Poznan, Poland, 1998), *Returned, Frescati* (Stockholm, 1998), *Returned, Parc de Buttes-Chaumont* (Paris, 1999), and *Returned, Galopptoio* (Villa Borghese, Rome, 1999).

4. "The volcano had for some years been a major Neapolitan attraction and a source of inspiration for the artist, and the spectacular volcanic activity of 1771 was recorded by many travelers on the Grand Tour." Susan Wise, Larry J. Feineberg, et al, *French and British Paintings from 1600 to 1800 in The Art Institute of Chicago: A Catalogue of the Collection* (Chicago: The Art Institute of Chicago, 1996).

5. Conversation between Matts Leiderstam and Friedeman Malsch, from the catalogue for the exhibition "Arkipelag," a project organized by Stockholm Cultural Capital, 1998.

Artist Project

Matts Leiderstam

View

North Dock, Bear Mountain State Park
Boscobel Restoration, Garrison
Great Chain Overlook, West Point Military Academy

View from *Boscobel Restoration*, Garrison

When we go for a stroll or choose to settle somewhere, we often look for a place with a view. Every city and country has places whose beauty is considered so great and unusual that we go there as tourists just to see them, and we remember them through the pictures we take or the postcards we buy. World-famous places have been seen, painted, and photographed from the same spots for generations.

Matts Leiderstam's paintings and sculptural works have examined the search for the picturesque and sublime within the eighteenth- and nine-teenth-century landscape painting tradition. For *Watershed*, Leiderstam will focus on the views of the Hudson River School painters. He will create a group of sculptural binoculars fitted with colored lenses fashioned after Claude Lorrain glasses (named after the French landscape painter). These will be situated to locate the landscape paintings of Thomas Cole, Frederick E. Church, Asher B. Durand, and Jasper F. Cropsey in such places as Bear Mountain, Garrison, and West Point. The lenses will rotate throughout the day, inviting viewers to revisit these landscapes through differing light conditions of blue, pink-brown, golden brown, and black. Three binoculars will be located directly across the Hudson River from each other so that the viewer-voyeur can also become an object of scrutiny. Leiderstam's project will also be published as a book, to be distributed internationally.

Christian Philipp Müller

Rhea Anastas

In 1999 the largest Swiss media conglomerate, Ringier AG, commissioned Christian Phillip Müller to produce an artist's project to accompany their corporate annual report. What he offered the company was an annual report as a work of art. Traveling to every major Ringier outpost during the fall of 1999, including locations in Asia and Eastern Europe, Müller supplemented the requisite statistical representations of the company—i.e., bar graphs and pie charts—with dozens of color snapshots and excerpts from his travel diary. Alongside the accounts on cash flow, income from electronic media, and the costs of paper stock and ink, for example, the report showed an image of glistening Slovakian sausages, as well as one editor's comment on how women's magazines reflect the changing goals of women in her country: "30 years ago most girls dreamed of becoming famous singers, 20 years ago actors, and 10 years ago models. Today's goal is solid professional training and a secure future."[1] The report further evidenced the artist's social mobility, which gave him access to the company's highest level actors, such as the Swiss ambassador to Vietnam, who served the artist fine Swiss wine upon their meeting (and who keeps a pet monkey), as well as to lower level employees, like the courier Müller accompanied to the company's printing facilities, and the editor in Prague who showed off her pet tarantula. Thus, under the artist's design supervision, the conventional high gloss corporate document became permeated by a surplus of alternative information and subjective impressions. The result is an "annual report-cum-travel diary,"[2] an idiosyncratic and fragmentary "portrait" of differences of social class, ethnicity, nationality, and gender which serves to perforate the monolithic identity of the Swiss-owned multinational corporate "empire."

Müller's labor in this project might be hard to distinguish from that of a journalist, a human resources consultant, a designer, or a sociologist. After all, it is based on facts and observations gathered through interviews with company managers and employees, and via tours of their facilities and work spaces. Yet Müller's gaze, while no less distanced, differs from the anthropological or sociological gaze in that its object does not readily conform to instrumental uses. The heterogeneity and excess of information pressure clear categorizations, while the apparent objectivity of scientific observation is replaced by a self-conscious aesthetic presentation combining visual and narrative elements. It is precisely this form of subterfuge that affords Müller a special status and occasion for commentary.

The type of aesthetic work Müller has practiced for over fifteen years is collaborative, interdisciplinary, and site-specific or contextual.[3] Müller treats art institutions (or other kinds of institutions like Ringier) not merely as neutral containers for the presentation of works of art but as historically, materially, and symbolically specific frames of reference and influence. As such Müller's practice can be seen to take a sociological approach to the field of art. The "business" of art—from the site of production in the studio to the sites of display and distribution in galleries, collections, museums, corporations, auction houses, magazines, and catalogues—is itself made the object of inquiry. Thus the institutional site or context for the work, which might be a literal place or a virtual location within a historical-archival, discursive, or representational context, is a primary agent in both informational and formal aspects of Müller's work.

Disciplinary boundaries are often breached in Müller's practice. Trained in design and the fine arts, Müller frequently draws links between the fields of architecture, design, the visual arts, and literature when analyzing a given context. In The Campus as a Work of Art (1996-98), a project commissioned by the public developer of the University of Lüneburg, Germany, Müller conducted a seminar with students and faculty over two semesters on the subject of campus planning and campus art in order to pose questions to the community about the relationship between aesthetics and educational ideals.[4] While his research process doubled as pedagogy, Müller's two-part material results were of a graphical nature. A series of 101 silkscreens featured paired campus plans, each one superimposing Lüneburg's plan in red with a second plan in beige drawn from the seminar's research on over 100 international campuses. The plans in each silkscreen were aligned according to the location of the library on each campus and organized along fifteen thematic categories, such as "Alma Maters of Germany's Post-War Chancellors and Presidents" and "Universities as the Wellspring of Social and Political Change."[5] The second part of the project, Department of Prototypes (1998), produced in collaboration with students, consisted of displays of over 200 prototypes for merchandise branded with a new logo of University of Lüneburg designed by the artist. The physical display of the prototypes—ranging from the traditional college sweatshirt to mouse pads and cutlery—in a former porter's office could only be viewed through the windows of the permanently closed building, just as the website was also designed for browsing only. The physical inaccessibility of the prototypes on display reflected the highly symbolic functioning of the logo-emblazened products as identity markers for the young university as it assumes many of the characteristics of transnational corporations in the competitive atmosphere of the global academic village.[6]

For artists like Müller, who inherit the lessons of the industrialized, mediated, and intellectualized

Christian Philipp Müller, *Ringier Annual Report*, 1999.

procedures of minimalism, pop, and conceptual art, the work of art often takes on ephemeral forms more akin to a process or an event than a handcrafted object, a shift which challenged the traditional premium put on the expressive gesture of the artist. The powerful role society grants to the artist, now displaced onto the effects of persona and rhetoric, continues to be another important area of critical inquiry in Müller's work. In his thesis exhibition at the Düsseldorf Kunstakademie in February 1986, Müller donned the uniform of a museum guard (not an uncommon job for an art student) and performed a gallery tour on the history of an absent set of paintings (the royal collection of the city's art school). Doubling as a lecture on reception his-tory and the sociology of taste, Müller delivered the talk while his audience actually viewed the latest works of Müller's classmates.

During the same period, Müller produced, through the city's tourism bureau, an artwork-as-tour entitled *Carl Theodor's Garden in Düsseldorf-Hellerhof*. Conducted by a team that included the artist dressed in a bow tie and suit and trailed by three musicians, this tour of unrealized monuments to celebrated figures from the history of philosophy, such as Diderot and Rousseau, involved narrative projections of an archaeology of the past onto existing sites. The tour described the plan of an eighteenth-century garden and palace designed by Nicolas de Pigage for Elector Carl Theodor, which had been proposed for a site that had become a banal contemporary suburban development. The performed tour served to highlight the historicity of notions of natural beauty and the key role of the artist as an arbiter of distinctions of taste and class.

Of the many cultural guises that Müller has adopted in the course of his work since the mid-1980s, his 1997 project *A Balancing Act*, for the venerable German exhibition institution of documenta, is perhaps the most powerful statement the artist has made on the subject of the artistic persona and its institutional stature.[7] Responding to curator Catherine David's historical and archival approach to documenta X, Müller chose to examine the history of two site-specific artworks from past documenta exhibitions: Walter de Maria's *The Vertical Earth/Kilometer* (1977) and Joseph Beuys' *7000 Oaks* (1982-87). In the performance part of the project, Müller adopted the uniform and mute persona of Philippe Petit, a French tightrope walker who famously traversed a line between the twin towers of New York City's World Trade Center in 1974. Placing his own artistic identity between two artistic father figures, Müller (as Petit) literally walked a line on the grounds of the Friedrichsplatz, emphasizing both the physical displacement of the de Maria and Beuys works caused by a redesign of the plaza in 1996 and the symbolic spectrum that the two works mark as canonical examples of the diametrically opposed lines of modernist art—formalist and political. The duality of this artistic inheritance was further emphasized in the half-oak, half-brass sculptural prop that Müller used as a balancing bar during the performance. The range of forms that constitute *A Balancing Act*—the sculptural prop, a display of documentation pertaining to the historical works of de Maria and Beuys, and a performance which was seen by most as a video document—underscored both the fragility of physical works of art and their status in the institution. The work's condition as a

Christian Phillip Müller, *A Balancing Act*, 1997, Performance and installation, documenta X.

set of physical traces—archival, sculptural, and performative—served also to emphasize the historical changes to the *work* of art, the very forms of artistic labor in which institutional and historical frames have come to figure so prominently in the aesthetic field. *A Balancing Act* suggested that the artistic persona, and perhaps ultimately art's function and critical potential, is a multiple personality, equal parts spectacle, parody, and vulnerability. ●

126

1. Christian Philipp Müller, diary entry "Bratislava, September 1999," *VOYAGE*, Ringuer Annual Report 1999 (Zurich: Ringier AG, 2000), 28.
2. Michael Ringier, the company's CEO, coined this term for Müller's project in his address to the readers of the report. Ibid., 8.
3. On the uses of the term site specificity in recent art, see Miwon Kwon, "One Place After Another: Notes on Site Specificity," *October* 80 (Spring 1997): 85-110.
4. Müller's project for the university, exemplifying his sociological approach, took the occasion of the young university's move to a new consolidated campus in a former military barracks on the edge of town to raise a series of questions on the ways the identity and intellectual pursuits of an academic community is shaped by the physical conditions and ideals that constitute the "campus" in a broad architectural, historical, and cultural context. See Christian Philipp Müller, *The Campus as a Work of Art: Art, Architecture, Design, Politics of Identity*, Beatrice von Bismarck, Diethelm Stoller, Astrid Wege, and Ulf Wuggenig, eds. (Düsseldorf: Richter Verlag, 2001).
5. Texts for each of the fifteen university categories were written by cultural theorist Astrid Wege and were displayed with the silkscreens throughout the University's library.
6. For more on this phenomenon, see the remarks of Ulf Wuggenig and Masao Miyoshi in *The Campus as a Work of Art*.
7. See George Baker and Christian Philipp Müller, "A Balancing Act," and George Baker, "On Christian Philipp Müller's *A Balancing Act*," *October* 82 (Fall 1997): 95-113, 114-118.

OPPOSITE Christian Phillip Müller, Installation in the library and building 7 of *The Campus as a Work of Art*, 1986, Mixed media, University of Lüneburg, Germany.

Artist Project

Christian Philipp Müller

Bard College
Annandale-on-Hudson

Hudson Valley Tastemakers

Trained in design and fine arts, Christian Philipp Müller frequently draws links between the fields of architecture, design, visual arts, culinary arts, and literature. Recent collaborative public projects include *A world of its own* in Vienna, *The Campus as a Work of Art* at the University of Lüneburg, and *Projet Unité* in Firmany, France.

Müller's project, *Hudson Valley Tastemakers*, will examine the specific tastes resulting from the changing nature, soil, and climate of the Hudson Valley. This project is developed collaboratively with Hudson Valley farmers, herbalists, and chefs from Columbia, Green, Dutchess, Orange, Putnam, and Ulster counties.

Earthsculpture

The sculpture will take the form of a soil collection. Six long ramps, each about four feet wide, will represent the different soil qualities of the Hudson Valley. Soil samples will be collected from excavation sites, in Columbia, Green, Dutchess, Orange, Putnam, and Ulster counties. Spontaneous vegetation will be allowed to develop and will be analyzed. Soil will be routinely overturned to show fresh color. A small area will be covered by a greenhouse to grow specific herbs in larger numbers before being planted outside.

Cookbook

The cookbook will include research on the distinct tastes of the Hudson Valley, including farm-raised and wild edible plants, such as mushrooms, berries, and herbs. It will also include portraits of outstanding farmers, restaurants, and food personalities. Interviews with chefs and students at the Culinary Institute of America will also be included.

SALSIFY OR OYSTER PLANT

20 DAYS. ROOTS TASTE LIKE FRIED OYSTERS
WHEN SLICED AND FRENCH FRIED. YOU CAN
ENJOY THEM ALL WINTER BY COVERING
PLANTS WITH STRAW OR LEAF MULCH IN
THE FALL. SHOOTS THAT START IN WINTER
GIVE SALADS A NICE FLAVOR. AN UNUSUAL
VEGETABLE DELICACY. EDIBLE FLOWERS.

Photograph of George Trakas, Hudson River waterfront

George Trakas

Patricia C. Phillips

In *Landscape and Memory*, Simon Schama explores the richness of river metaphors and the "makers and consumers of fluvial myth."[1] He examines how rivers have offered redemptive, nationalistic, and other inspiring metaphors throughout history. In 1838, for instance, Thomas Babington Macaulay, member of British Parliament, on a visit to the Rhone River, was inspired to write: "Rivers have…the appearance of animation, something resembling character. They are sometimes slow and dark-looking, sometimes fierce and impetuous, sometimes bright and dancing and almost flippant. [The Rhone] is a vehement and rapid stream. It seems cheerful and full of animal spirits."[2] These spirited reactions to the French river undoubtedly were shaped by his experiences of London's Thames River and its more temperate disposition. Schama writes: "the Thames was not only a balm for political friction; it was also a winding ribbon that bound together all ranks and conditions, mean and mighty, plebeian and patrician, in a single, indivisible community. A poetic cruise along its course supplied scene after scene of perfect social concordance."[3]

Historical and contemporary descriptions of the Hudson River are numerous, but a general impression situates this major river somewhere between the quixotic volatility of the Rhone and the calm beneficence of the Thames. It is the river that captivated Thomas Cole, Frederick Church, Asher Durand, and others to capture its metaphysical qualities in the brush strokes, pigments, and luminosity of painting. But the character of the Hudson also has an unquestionably prosaic quality. According to Schama, "the Hudson Valley painters had to navigate carefully between the savagery of 'wild' scenery and the mechanical clutter of the industrial river."[4] The Hudson is, in other words, a site of inspiration and utility.

The Hudson is an active, working river. On a typical day—a century ago as well as today—ferries, ships, and barges travel up and down the river under their own power or pushed and pulled by tugs. Industries and corporations exploit its thrilling force to generate electricity and other commodities while often polluting and compromising its finely balanced ecology. Like so many rivers, the Hudson

George Trakas, *Curach and Bollard*, 2000, Pier 26, Hudson River Park

"On a typical day…ferries, ships, and barges travel up and down the river… Industries and corporations exploit its thrilling force togenerate electricity and other commodities while often polluting and compromising its finely balanced ecology…. The Hudson reflects enduring conflicts and ambiguities between natural systems and human expectations, ecology and culture, the past and the future. It is in this relentless stream, simultaneously exploited and celebrated by human beings, that George Trakas finds a fruitful place to work."

reflects enduring conflicts and ambiguities between natural systems and human expectations, ecology and culture, the past and the future. It is in this relentless stream, simultaneously exploited and celebrated by human beings, that George Trakas finds a fruitful place to work.

Trakas has lived by the Hudson River most of his adult life. In his studio in lower Manhattan is an elegantly simple wood frame and linen skiff that he can hoist over his shoulders and carry several blocks to the river. In this small, maneuverable craft, he has studied the river and its sweeping intricacies throughout the seasons for many years. And through his many years of observation—becoming intimately familiar with the river intellectually and somatically—a broad and eclectic knowledge of the dynamic dimensions of the Hudson has congealed into a spare, intensely focused aesthetic vision.

A good example of his honed and modest tactics is his recent project, *Curach and Bollard* (2000), for Pier 26 in New York City. Like sutures that connect the riverfront to the water, the edge of Manhattan once had a procession of sturdy piers that extended from the tip of the island to midtown. Once utilitarian sites, many of the piers have become obsolete, deteriorating and tumbling into the water, leaving behind thickets of vertical posts. (In recent times, some of the piers have been reclaimed for recreational and other uses.) Sponsored by Minetta Brook, Trakas constructed a seating area on the south side of Pier 26, screened overhead by two inverted wood frame hulls of old boats. *Curach and Bollard* further provided steps leading down to a waterfront platform where people could fish and disembark from canoes and kayaks. Using vernacular industrial and nautical materials and artifacts, Trakas created a diminutive, flexible site that allows people to get physically close to the river. It is a simple objective with significant implications.

In 1999, the Dia Center for the Arts, a multidisciplinary arts organization that will open a museum in Beacon in spring 2003, and Scenic Hudson, a non-profit environmental organization dedicated to enhancing the Hudson River Valley, commissioned Diane Shamash, Executive Director of Minetta Brook, and Trakas to study and make recommendations for the Beacon waterfront. The resulting report, *The Beacon Waterfront: A Survey of the Edge*, presents the problems and possibilities of the three-mile long waterfront. It is a physical plan for enhanced access to the Hudson as well as a proposal for ways that artists might engage the Beacon waterfront. The report focuses on Beacon Landing, the harbor area, Denning's Point State Park, Fishkill Creek, Madam Brett Park, and the Beacon Terminal area.

Trakas is now at work on Beacon Landing, a small peninsula south of Newburgh-Beacon Bridge owned by Scenic Hudson. Commissioned by Dia Center for the Arts, Scenic Hudson, and Minetta Brook, he seeks to make a more accessible waterfront out of a long-neglected site. All but abandoned except for by those who fish, or by teenagers who party late at night, Beacon Landing was once a robust and active hub. For many years train lines converged here. Freight cars were loaded onto barges and shipped across the river to Newburgh and the freight line that traveled the length of the river on the west side. The construction of the Newburgh-Beacon Bridge and other changes in the region and its industries made the landing obsolete.

Ignored and overlooked, Beacon Landing is currently an unruly and overgrown eyesore. Walking the site with the artist in early summer, Trakas impressed me as an eloquent and enthusiastic guide. Pointing out old, partially buried tracks and ties, pieces of metal and cinder, and other detritus, he constructed a vivid history of the site that informs his view of the future. Rejecting and condemning a generic waterfront design of an ambitious architecture of grand promenades and predictable amenities that actually distance people from any direct experience of the river, Trakas plans to construct a series of paths and platforms that stabilize the site and bring people into close contact with it.

A self-taught engineer, builder, and ecologist, the artist's first tasks at Beacon Landing have been to clear areas that open up paths and vistas to the water. On the north side of the peninsula is a deteriorating bulkhead that Trakas will rebuild and stabilize. A practical, if not essential, objective, the bulkhead also serves as a metaphor. It is a spinal column which is indispensable to the viability of the site. Clearing passages of the site, navigating his small boat around the perimeter of the peninsula, or devising ways to fasten decaying concrete platforms from the old train landing to create fishing and seating areas, Trakas' methodology is a calculated balance of planning and fortuity.

The process is intense and yet unhurried. It takes time to know a place. Research and development, observation and creation, seeing and making, are not distinct and linear activities. Like the most pervasive fluvial metaphor, the work is about circulation. Trakas' most reliable guides and creative resources are the existing conditions of a site. His process neither ignores nor eradicates the physical evidence of industrial development, natural erosion, or the interventions of people who have used the site in sanctioned or clandestine ways. Constantly shifting from the detail to the panoramic, from the singular to the systemic, Trakas embraces time as a synthetic medium to connect the past and future, the social and physical landscapes.

To return to Schama: "the impact of humanity on the earth's ecology has not been an unmixed blessing, neither has the long relationship between nature and culture been an unrelieved and predetermined calamity."[5] Perhaps this observation touches on the most salient dimension of Trakas' work. The relationship of nature and culture is complicatedly reciprocal. We need not wring our hands in dismay with the use of natural sites nor proceed unthinkingly with voracious development. But we need to see. And ultimately, we need to act. Trakas' work doesn't offer an idealized distant view. We may barely recognize that his interventions are there, but they place us directly in the here and now. •

1. Simon Schama, *Landscape and Memory* (London: Harper Collins, 1995), 362-63.
2. Ibid., 355.
3. Ibid., 356.
4. Ibid., 364.
5. Ibid., 9-10.

View looking south towards *Beacon Landing*

View of *Pier 26*, 1999

View of *Beacon Landing*, 2002

George Trakas

Beacon Landing Project

George Trakas has devoted the past twenty years to creating environmental sculptures that often take the form of bridges, pathways, and docks. His interest in water resource issues, tides, currents, and shoreline construction is manifest in a wide range of projects from *Berth Haven* at the headquarters of the National Oceanic and Atmospheric Administration in Seattle, Washington, to *Sword Bridge* in Thiers, France.

Trakas' *Beacon Landing Project* will involve the shoreline stabilization of 2,500 feet of shoreline, and the construction of a new public park at Beacon Landing. This art work will include decks, dock areas, and stairways to the water, as well as a community boathouse and landing for small vessels. This public art work will also include a handicapped-access fishing pier and granite steps that will increase safe public access to the peninsula and prevent further deterioration of the edge around the entire 26-acre site. Trakas' project is part of the larger redevelopment of Beacon Landing, which includes a mixed-use development with a hotel and conference center, restaurant and offices, and is being developed to increase public access and involvement with Beacon's waterfront. This art work resulted from a collaborative planning process with representatives from Dia Center for the Arts, Scenic Hudson, Minetta Brook, the City of Beacon, New York State Parks Department, and Central Hudson Gas and Electric.

UPPER AND LOWER LEFT
George Trakas, *Curach and Bollard*,
2000, Pier 26, Hudson River Park.

UPPER RIGHT
Pier 26, original condition of site.

George Trakas, *Beacon Point Model*, 2002.

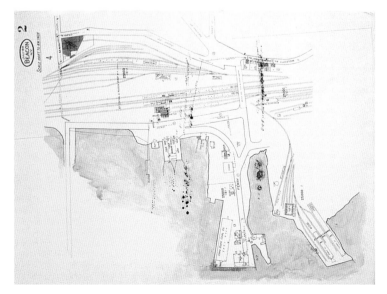

Historical photograph of
Beacon Landing.

James Welling, *Brussels*, 1994, 27 x 34 inches.

James Welling

Alain Cueff

One of the works included in James Welling's recent survey exhibition (traveled to The Wexner Center, Baltimore Museum of Art, Los Angeles Museum of Contemporary Art, 2000-2001) was *Ashes*, a 1974 video showing three sequences of shots of a pile of ashes being barely stirred by a gentle draft. Although he has used this medium only on rare occasions, choosing to concentrate on photography very early in his career, *Ashes* nonetheless prefigures many key aspects of his overall oeuvre. At first, we are struck by the strange temporality of the image. Nothing, or nearly nothing, moves or changes in this tightly-framed shot, nothing "progresses"; our gaze remains caught in a time that does not pass, or from which we feel excluded since no visual or narrative event marks its flow. In fact, what we are faced with is the very *time* of the image, an indefinite time unfamiliar to our habits, but through which the image manages to exist and endure, continuing unceasingly to present itself. By going against the rules of a technology that is primarily designed to capture and render movement in its immediacy, by presenting a video as if it were a photograph, by ultimately transforming the former into the latter, *Ashes* reveals that the goal of Welling's art is not simply to fix an image of what has been (with the past reaching us only as a relic), but rather in producing images with neither a beginning nor an end. Welling's work opens on to memory wherein the past and history assert themselves in a living continuum of the present.

Some of the photographic series are particularly exemplary in this regard. *Diary of Elizabeth C. Dixon, 1840-1841/Connecticut Landscapes* (1977-86), for instance, juxtaposes details of pages from a nineteenth-century private journal with photographs of New England winter landscapes dating from over a hundred years later. Here, the past is neither suspended nor depicted: it is lived out in its continuity, empathetically. It is not presented to us as a mere document; it is free of both its personal and conceptual dimensions. The relation between the journal pages with their indecipherable writing (some with flowers and leaves tucked into them), and the views of the New England forests is at once formal and

sensible, explicit and implicit. They call for neither a conclusion nor a resolution: they construct a poetic space unlimited by boundaries. The series *Buildings by H. H. Richardson, 1838-1886* (1988-94) works in a more obvious manner: all the photographs present details of different Richardson buildings like so many pieces of a jigsaw puzzle. The part and the whole, as well as the present and history, exist in a relation that, while being allusive and metaphorical, is also very close.

Just as Richardson's buildings mark a moment just prior to the emergence of modernist architecture, Welling's series on railways (1987-94), lace factories (1993), and the industrial sites of Wolfsburg (1994) similarly capture cultures and artifacts marking the transition from the nineteenth to the twentieth century, from one world to another. Far from being abandoned, however, these places remain inhabited, contemporary, and alive in Welling's photographs, running counter to more nostalgic views of the past. The railways, the locomotives, the looms, and the spaces given over to industrial production do not belong in a museum of obsolete traditions but remain instruments of an active economy and vital actors in landscapes that they have profoundly shaped over many years. What has been, remains. What once lived, lives still, and this life is exactly what Welling takes up as a photographer. Which is to say, the subject of his works is not what one literally sees in his images (i.e., a metal bridge, smoking chimneys), but what one recognizes as the present-day experience of history that is both

James Welling, *Diary of Elizabeth and James Dixon, (1840-41), Connecticut Landscapes*, 1977-86, Silver print, 3^1/$_2$ x 4^1/$_2$ inches.

of the world and of the gaze through which it is envisioned.

Contrary to what its ubiquity may lead us to think, photography is not a simple and faithful reproduction of the real. It entails the construction of a gaze that questions appearances in order to articulate them as forms. Welling's art is not solely a matter of taking photographs. Above all, it is about continually reconsidering the gaze, that is to say, not only choosing among various prints those which may effectively become strong individual images but interpreting them as parts within an ensemble. This is the case with the works mentioned already, as well as with the *Light Sources* series (1992-98). Light is the common denominator in the photographs of landscapes, architectural elements, objects, and animals that make up this series, produced after a re-reading of *Los Angeles Architecture* (1976-78) in which light dominates as a motif. As the basic element of photosensitivity, light endows the visible with a sculptural dimension, and, at the same time, acquires its own plastic autonomy. To put it bluntly, light contributes to the visibility or creation of forms and does so much more essen-

tially than any concrete material. "What you see isn't what you really get. There is something else—the effect of photography," Welling has said. It is through this gap between recognition and feeling, seeing and understanding, apprehending and imagining that art infiltrates photography.

Photography does not prescribe what is there to be seen; it establishes the conditions of a possible image, even when the systems of recognition and identification are in abeyance. It is possible to consider Welling's series of abstract works from this angle, including *Tile Photographs* (1985), *New Abstractions* (2000), and *Gelatin Photographs* (1984) and *Untitled (Aluminum Foil)*, 1980-1981. This last series, which shows crumpled aluminum in various states, its contours modulated by the light, bears an obvious formal relation to *Ashes*, just as the *New Abstractions* recall the *Railroad Photographs*. However, it would be a mistake to look for direct, demonstrable links between the "figurative" and "abstract" works. For Welling, abstraction is not the result of a theoretical decision or a historical a priori. Rather, it is the issue, or, if you prefer, the heritage of light. ●

James Welling, *Diary of Elizabeth and James Dixon, (1840-41), Connecticut Landscapes*, 1977-86, Silver print, 3³/₈ x 4³/₈ inches.

James Welling, *Gelatin Photograph 45*, 1984, Silver print, 16 x 20 inches.

James Welling, *Norfolk Southern SD40-2, Oak Island, N.J.*, 1991, Unique silver print, 18 x 22 inches.

Agricultural Works

James Welling's photographic subjects include landscapes, railroad yards, and nineteenth-century architecture by H.H. Richardson. His recent works have been exhibited at the Palais des Beaux-Arts in Brussels, the Wexner Center for the Arts in Columbus, the Baltimore Museum of Art, and the Museum of Contemporary Art in Los Angeles.

James Welling's project, *Agricultural Works*, includes photographs and audio recordings about agriculture in the greater Hudson Valley. The project will document farmland, crops, livestock, vineyards, farm architecture, machinery and tools in the counties north of New York City. *Agricultural Works* has been developed collaboratively with Will Welling, the photographer's brother, a musician living in the Albany area. Will Welling will perform original and traditional fiddle tunes with background recordings of farm machinery. *Agricultural Works* will be exhibited in university galleries throughout the Hudson Valley. It will also be published as a book of photographs, sheet music and a compact disc.

OPPOSITE James Welling, *Agricultural Works*, 2002.

Olana State Historic Site, Hudson

Boscobel Restoration, Garrison

ISBN: 0-9723220-0-0

© 2002 Minetta Brook
105 Hudson Street, No. 411
New York, NY 10013
www.minettabrook.org

Please address all inquiries to
Minetta Brook
105 Hudson Street, No. 411
New York, NY 10013
e-mail: watershed@minettabrook.org

Editor: Miwon Kwon

Translators: Mike Garner, Charles Penwarden
and Peter Samuelsson

Graphic Design: Dan Miller Design, New York

Typeface: Franklin Gothic

Printed in Hong Kong

Front and back cover: Great Chain Overlook,
West Point Military Academy, West Point
Photos: Andrew Cross

Photo credits:
Lothar Baumgarten: 76, 78-81
Matthew Buckingham: 90, 92-93
Andrew Cross: 1, 2-9, 10-11, 12, 18-24, 26-27,
35-36, 100, 103, 118, 154-160
Matts Leiderstam: 159
Annea Lockwood: 28 (top)
Christian Phillip Müller: 25, 28 (bottom), 56, 59,
120, 128, 130-131
Pae White: 31
The Science Museum, London, England: 112
ART ON FILE: 40, 41

View from *Great Chain Overlook*, West Point Military Academy

View from *Boscobel Restoration*, Garrison